EXAMINING RELIGIONS

Roman Catholic Christianity

Clare Richards

Heinemann

NIHIL OBSTAT and IMPRIMATUR
The Reverend Nicholas Kearney, MA, STM
Censor for East Anglia Diocese

6 October, 1994

The *nihil obstat* and *imprimatur* are official declarations that a book or pamphlet is free of doctrinal and moral error. No implication is contained therein that those who have granted the *nihil obstat* and *imprimatur* agree with the contents, opinions, or statements expressed.

Heinemann Educational Publishers
Halley Court, Jordan Hill, Oxford OX2 8EJ

MADRID ATHENS PARIS
FLORENCE PRAGUE WARSAW
PORTSMOUTH NH CHICAGO SAO PAULO
SINGAPORE TOKYO MELBOURNE AUCKLAND
IBADAN GABORONE JOHANNESBURG

© Clare Richards, 1995

First published 1995

99 98 97 96 95
10 9 8 7 6 5 4 3 2 1

British Library Cataloguing in Publication Data

A catalogue record for this book is available from the British Library

ISBN 0 435 30318 X
Designed and typeset by Gecko Ltd, Bicester, Oxon
Illustrated by Barry Rowe and Gill Bishop
Printed and bound in Spain by Mateu Cromo

Acknowledgements

The publishers would like to thank W Owen Cole, our religious studies consultant.

The publishers would like to thank the following for permission to reproduce copyright material.
The Aberdeen *Press and Journal* for the extract from an article by Bishop Mario Conti on p. 109; David Alton MP for his words taken from *Seek Ye First* on p. 106; Ampleforth College, York, for the extract from the school prospectus on p. 67; Clare Banyard for the quotation on p. 72, taken from *Catholic Women*, Summer 1994; H Bauer Publishing Ltd for the extract from *Take a Break* magazine on p. 100; the Bible Societies/HarperCollins Publishers Ltd, UK © American Bible Society, 1966, 1971, 1976, 1992, for the extracts from the *Good News Bible* throughout the book; CAFOD for the extracts on pp. 50 and 64; Cassell plc for the extracts from *Celebrating Resistance* by Dorothee Soelle on pp. 91 and 120 and the extract from *Praying Together in Words and Song* by Taizé on p. 59 including the music to *Adoramus te Domine*, reproduced by permission of the publisher, also for the extracts, throughout the book, from *The Catechism of the Catholic Church*, 1994, published by Geoffrey Chapman; Catholic Media Office for the extracts from *Briefing* on pp. 43 and 103 (the words of Pope John Paul II) and on p. 67 (the words of Pablo Cassals), 106 (Declaration, 1974), 115 (pastoral letter of Bishop Brewer), 120 (text from the *Inter Faith Network*); the Catholic National Religious Vocation Centre for the description of vocation on p. 85; Christian Action Research & Education for the extract from *Make Love Last*, a secondary school sex education video and teachers' pack, sponsored by CARE (available from 'Make Love Last', PO BOX 137, Middlesbrough, Cleveland TS5 4BR) on p. 105; Christian Aid for the

extract on p. 92; CTS for the extract from *Tomorrows' Parish* by Adrian Smith on p. 90; Darton Longman and Todd Ltd for the extracts from the *Jerusalem Bible*, published and copyright 1966, 1967 and 1968 by Darton Longman and Todd Ltd and Doubleday & Co Inc, and used by permission of the publishers, on pp. 40 (*Peter 2:9*) and 119 (*1 Timothy 6:10*), also for the extract from *Good Friday People* by Sheila Cassidy, published and copyright 1991 by Darton Longman and Todd Ltd, on p. 26, for the extracts from *Sacraments* by Hugh Lavery, published and copyright 1982 by Darton Longman and Todd Ltd, on pp. 29 and 47, and for the extract from *Jesus Before Christianity* by Albert Nolan, published and copyright 1976 by Darton Longman and Todd Ltd, on p. 15, all used by permission of the publishers; Faber & Faber Ltd for the words of Dennis Potter on p. 121; HarperCollins Publishers Ltd for the short quotation from *Hope and Suffering* by Archbishop Desmond Tutu, 1984, on p. 114, for the extracts from *A Gift from God* by Mother Teresa of Calcutta, 1975, on pp. 31, 63, 106, and for the extract from *Our Faith Story* by A Patrick Purnell, 1985, on p. 80; Cardinal Basil Hume for the extract from an article 'AIDS: Time for Moral Renaissance' on p. 101; International Commission on English in the Liturgy Inc for excerpts quoted throughout the book from the English translation of *The Roman Missal* © 1973, ICEL, from *Pastoral Care of the Sick: Rites of Anointing and Viaticum* © 1982, ICEL, from the English translation of *A Book of Prayers* © 1982, ICEL, and from the *Order of Christian Funerals* © 1985, ICEL, all rights reserved (English translations of *Apostles' Creed* and *Nicene Creed* by the International Consultation on English Texts); Bill Jones for the poem on p. 11; Libreria Edtrice Vaticana for the extract from *The Interpretation of the Bible in the Church* on p. 80; Kevin Mayhew Publishers for the extract from *To Grow in Christ* by Damian Lundy, 1980, on p. 24, for the adapted extract from *Prayers for Peacemakers* by V Flessati, 1988, on p. 25, for the extracts from *Focus on Sacraments* by Peter Wilkinson, 1987, on pp. 35 (words of Pope Paul VI), 36, 39, 41 (the words of Pope John Paul II), and for the extract from *The Rosary for Children* by H J Richards, 1988, (poem by Marie Noel) on p. 53; Anna McKenzie for her poem on p. 74; Newspaper Publishing plc for extracts from *The Independent and Independent on Sunday* on pp. 65, 84 (paraphrased), 105, 107 (adapted); Father Harry O'Carroll and the Columban Fathers for the extract on p. 33; Penguin Books Ltd for the extract from *Pensèes* by Blaise Pascal, translated by A J Krailsheimer (Penguin Classics, 1966), © A J Krailsheimer 1966, on p. 84; Michael and Terri Quinn for the extract from *How to prepare your children for Mass*, Veritas Family Resources, on p. 57; *The Tablet* for the extract from 'Hero of the sewers' by Maryanne Traylen, quoting the words of Jaime Jaramillo, on p. 71, for the extract from 'Viewpoint' by Sean McDonagh on p. 113, and for the extract on p. 115; Brian Wicker for the extract on p. 117.

The publishers would like to thank the following for permission to reproduce photographs.
David Alton 7 (bottom); Ampleforth College, York 66 (bottom); Andes Press Agency/Carlos Reyes-Manzo 6 (right), 11, 19, 30, 31, 38, 41, 45 (both), 48 (both), 55, 61 (right), 90; Andes Press Agency/Linea Press/Rino Bianchi 6 (left); Andes Press Agency/Maria Luiza M Carvalho 120; Bridgeman Art Library/Prado, Madrid 53; CAFOD 60, 65; Sandra Carr 34; Catholic Housing Aid Society 69; Cheshire Foundation 75 (left); Children of the Andes 71; Anthony Cooper 78; Courtauld Institute Galleries/Bridgeman Art Library 22; Anna Dimascio 25, 79; Diocesan Office, Roman Catholic Diocese of East Anglia 47, 95 (top left), 95 (right); John Dove 4; Eastern Counties Newspapers Ltd 89, 94; John Fisher 16, 32, 57, 95 (bottom left), 112, 119; Alex Frye 70 (bottom right); Sally and Richard Greenhill 20 (bottom), 68, 107; Robert Harding 28; 'Let the Children Live', Walsingham 70 (top right); Sister Maureen MacKenzie 85, 118; Tom Mackin 96 (left); Father Paul Maddison 67; Panos Pictures 23; Caroline Penn/Impact 82; Plymouth and Torbay Health Authority 75 (right); Linda Proud 12, 52, 86, 104; Rex 36, 59, 114; Bert Richards 17, 29, 56, 66 (top), 98; St Columban Fathers 33; St Vincent de Paul Society 96 (three photos in right column), 97; School of World Art Studies, University of East Anglia 81; Science Photo Library 110; Father Tony Sketch 15, 42, 50, 58, 61 (left); Frank Spooner Pictures/Richard Tomkins 72; Mark Spring 70 (right); UNICEF 7 (top); John Walmsley 14; Andy Warman 9; Zefa 5, 18, 20 (top), 26, 62, 88, 92, 108, 121.

Cover photographs by Andes Press Agency (left and bottom right) and Bert Richards (top right).

The publishers have made every effort to trace copyright holders. However, if any material has been incorrectly acknowledged, we would be pleased to correct this at the earliest opportunity.

> *This book is dedicated to all my pupils, past and present, who have taught me as much as I ever taught them.*
>
> *Clare Richards*

CONTENTS

1 INTRODUCTION

Cardinal Basil Hume welcomes the new Catechism

Quite recently, a book was published called *Catechism of the Catholic Church*. It became an immediate bestseller. In the photo, Cardinal Hume, the head of the **Roman Catholic** Church in England, has received his copy. The book was written by **Pope John Paul II** for his bishops and other teachers.

It records how the Catholic **Church** sees itself today. It is not the sort of book you would just pick up and read, but Catholics and others are interested to know what is in it. This book will explain something about that.

Roman Catholics are Christians, but not all Christians are Roman Catholics. Christians are followers of the first-century Jew, Jesus, whom they call 'The Christ'. 'The **Christ**' means 'The Chosen One of God'.

Like all Christians, Roman Catholics are ordinary people who see God's plans for the human race come to perfection in Jesus. He was a carpenter in a quiet village in Galilee, northern Palestine, 2000 years ago.

There are millions of Roman Catholics throughout the world. If you live in countries like Eire, Italy or Peru you and all your neighbours are likely to be Roman Catholics. But wherever you live, there will be a local Catholic church and it is sure to be filled several times over on a Sunday with Roman Catholic worshippers.

Families, young and old, rich and poor, black and white, famous and ordinary, attend church worship, called the **Mass,** every week. Not all Roman Catholics go to church regularly, but they still believe that Jesus, the Christ, is the best model they have, and the best insight into the mystery of God.

Like all groups of people, Roman Catholics have sometimes been misunderstood or misrepresented. They also have a less than perfect history. The Roman Catholic Church is made up of saints and sinners.

This book is about Catholics the world over. If you are a Roman Catholic, hopefully it will help you to understand your beliefs and practices more clearly and to appreciate other Christian denominations which share your ideals. If you are not a Catholic, this book should help you to understand Catholics – why, for example, a Catholic sportsman makes the sign of the cross as he runs onto the pitch; a woman lights candles before a statue of Mary; a Church leader calls for sexual restraint among young people today.

Look at the photographs on these pages. Are the faces familiar? They are Roman Catholics who sometimes make the headlines.

Pope John Paul II

The photo above shows the leader of the Roman Catholic Church today. He is Pope John Paul II, a Polish bishop who was elected Pope in 1978 and so lives in the Vatican in Rome. Born Karol Wojtyla, he became a **priest** in 1946, and 20 years later Archbishop of Krakow. He studied philosophy and moral theology and speaks many languages. In Poland he was outspoken against the Communist authorities of his day, but now he is well known for his strong teaching on traditional moral values. He has survived an assassination attempt.

Mother Teresa of Calcutta (right), founder of the **religious order** Missionaries of Charity, is probably one of the best-known Roman Catholics today. All over the world people respect and love this elderly Albanian **nun** who works, with her sister nuns, wherever there is poverty, neglect and tragedy. Born in 1910 in Yugoslavia, she became a nun in Dublin and later taught geography in Calcutta. In 1948 she started a new religious order to work with the destitute poor. Today, her sisters work in 60 countries, including Britain.

David Alton (opposite page) is the Liberal Democrat MP for Liverpool, Mossley Hill. He is known in politics as a tireless campaigner for the rights of the unborn child. As a Roman Catholic, he has inherited a strong attitude towards the sanctity of life from the moment of conception, and now heads the campaigns that express concern over the ease with which abortions can be obtained. He went to the Catholic Edmund Campion School in Hornchurch, Essex, and later to Christ's College of Education, Liverpool. He works alongside many caring agencies, such as Crisis for Christmas.

Mother Teresa

The Duchess of Kent on a UNICEF mission

David Alton MP, doing home repairs for an elderly constituent

Recently, the Duchess of Kent (above) made history by leaving the established Church of England to become a Catholic. It was an unusual step to take because members of the British royal family are the leading members of the Church of England. In fact, Roman Catholics have been barred from senior roles in government, and under present laws England could not have a Catholic monarch. The Duchess made a personal decision to join the Catholic Church as a result of working alongside Catholics and feeling 'at home' in their way of spiritual life. This movement between Churches is increasingly common among Christians today and shows how they are growing closer together.

FIND OUT

▶ Interview two or three Roman Catholics. They may be members of your family or pupils or teachers at your school. Ask them to tell you why they are Roman Catholic and what it means to them.

▶ Find out more about one of the well-known Catholics mentioned in this unit. Be prepared to talk to your class about them for five minutes.

You may be a Christian who is not a Roman Catholic; or you may be a Roman Catholic who has an Anglican or Orthodox friend. Why are there different Christian groups? The simple answer is that every tree spreads its branches in different directions. Christianity, like a tree, is living and growing. It has roots: St. Paul, an early Christian, said Christians are rooted and grounded in Christ.

'... and I pray that Christ will make his home in your hearts through faith. I pray that you may have your roots and foundation in love, so that you, together with all God's people, may have the power to understand how broad and long, how high and deep, is Christ's love.'

(Ephesians 3:17–18)

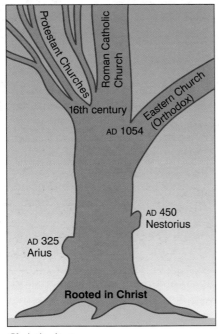

Christianity tree

The diagram shows how the Christianity tree has developed. Some churches branched out from the main trunk as early as the fifth century. As Christianity grew over the centuries and among people of different races, its development did not always take place smoothly. It was complicated by the fact that the Roman Empire had developed two centres, one in Rome and the other in Constantinople in the East. There was rivalry between Christians of East and West. In 1054 it came to a head and Rome and Constantinople broke away from each other. They each claimed the other side had branched off the main trunk.

By the mid-sixteenth century Christianity in the West was in further disarray as many individuals and groups protested against the growing power of Rome and against corruption among Church leaders. Protesters (protestants) such as Martin Luther and later John Calvin demanded reforms which were rejected. The split known as the Reformation followed. For personal and political reasons, the English King Henry VIII broke relations with the Roman Pope and in 1565 the Church of England called itself both Catholic and Reformed.

Date	Saint
	Peter
	Paul
AD 100	
AD 200	Irenaeus
AD 300	Athanasius
AD 400	Augustine
AD 500	Patrick
	Columba
	Benedict
AD 600	Gregory
	Aidan
AD 700	Bede
AD 800	
AD 900	Edmund, Martyr
AD 1000	Wenceslaus
	Anselm
	Margaret (Scotland)
AD 1100	
	Bernard of Clairvaux
	Thomas (Canterbury)
AD 1200	
	Francis of Assisi
	Clare of Assisi
	Dominic
AD 1300	
	Catherine of Siena
	Julian of Norwich
AD 1400	
AD 1500	Thomas More (b.1478)
	Ignatius Loyola
	Francis Xavier
	Teresa of Avila
AD 1600	
AD 1700	Vincent de Paul
	Cure d'Ars
	Julie Billiart
AD 1800	
	John Bosco
	John Henry Newman
	Teresa of Lisieux
AD 1900	
	Maximilian Kolbe
	Pope John XXIII
	Oscar Romero

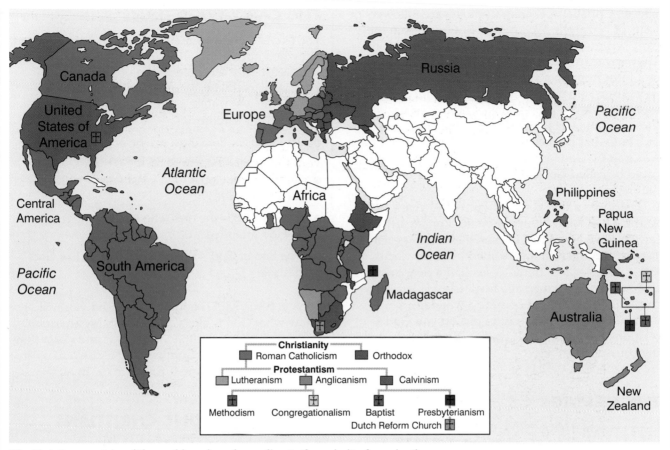

The Christian countries of the world – coloured according to the majority denomination

THE ROMAN CATHOLIC CHURCH

The Roman Catholic branch of the tree has always claimed to be the main trunk growing from the roots of Christianity. It has always been led by a Pope, elected at the death of the previous one. Pope John Paul II claims to be the present successor of St Peter himself (see p. 88).

The map shows the spread of Christianity. The Roman Catholic Church is the largest branch of Christianity. Numbers are difficult to assess, but it is estimated that the 960 million Roman Catholics worldwide represent 60 per cent of all Christians, and 18 per cent of the world's population.

THINGS TO DO

▶ This is a task for the class. With the help of books from the library, find out about one or two outstanding Catholics from each century. *The timeline gives suggestions.* Each member of the class should chose one person and write a short biography. Illustrate your work if possible and display it imaginatively.

Christianity, like a tree, is living and growing

9

Like all Christians, Roman Catholics are followers of Jesus of Nazareth. We know about Jesus from the early writers Paul, Mark, Matthew, Luke and John. They wrote in that order – Paul from about AD 55 and John from about AD 95. No one attempted to write Jesus' biography. The letters of Paul and the four **Gospels** are professions of faith in Jesus, i.e. these authors wrote not simply what Jesus said and did, but what he meant to them. They believed he was sent by God, and that he was so like God he could be called God's Son, sharing God's very nature.

Jesus was a first-century Jew. For 90 years, his country had been occupied by the Roman army. Jews believed God had chosen them as a special people. But the Romans seemed more powerful. What were Jews to think? Jesus had a clear answer, and he taught his message fearlessly. He left his carpenter's bench and became a wandering preacher, talking of his vision of God and God's relationship to people. It was a vision that changed the course of history.

THE MESSAGE

Jesus preached about God, not about himself. He talked about God's Kingdom or Rule over the World. As a Jew he used stories (called parables) to shock his listeners and make them think. The theme of his preaching was freedom – liberation. He told the people that they did not need freedom from Roman occupation so much as freedom from selfishness and hatred; from sickness of heart and body. He called on them to be forgiving and compassionate to one another, just as God is towards everyone.

THE RESULT OF JESUS' PREACHING

Strangely, Jesus found himself in trouble for teaching such Good News (**Gospel**). His message upset the religious authorities because he tended to put the 'spirit' of a law before the law itself. His popularity with the crowds did not help, even though he worked wonders for them, healing the sick of mind and body.

Jesus was eventually tried in a religious court for *blasphemy* (claiming Godly power) and then in a political court for *treason* against the Roman state. Jesus was put to death on a cross. But within days, his Jewish followers claimed he was more alive than ever. They began to speak out, claiming his presence was among them and his **Spirit** in them.

THE EARLY CHRISTIANS

The five early writers mentioned above were excited. They had not all known Jesus personally, but they enthusiastically accepted his values as their own. They struggled with words to write about him because he was unlike any human being they had known. They said he is:

- The Christ – the Chosen One of God, for whose coming the Jews had long prayed
- The Word of God – God's last word on the meaning of life
- The Saviour – the one who sets people free to be as God intended
- The Son of God – the one who is just like God himself.

Look at Jesus, said the five writers, and you will know what God is like. Christians today are those people who continue to look at Jesus and claim they know God. They say God has 'come down to us' in Jesus, or God has 'come through to us' in him.

ROMAN CATHOLIC CHRISTIANS

Roman Catholic Christians have a special affection for Simon Peter, the fisherman follower of Jesus. He was one of the twelve close friends or **apostles**, who accompanied Jesus when he preached in the towns and villages of Palestine. He was chosen by Jesus to lead the believers in preaching the new message. Peter means 'rock', the foundation on which the new community was built.

Roman Catholics see the Pope as continuing to exercise the leadership of Peter.

REFLECTION

Thou art Peter; and upon this rock I will build my church, and the gates of hell shall not prevail against it. And I will give to thee the keys of the kingdom of heaven.

(Matthew 16:18–19, Douay Version)

Peter was a fisherman

THINGS TO DO

▶ If someone you know showed an interest in the Catholic Church, how would you explain to them what a Roman Catholic Christian is?

▶ Imagine you are asked to write a short entry for *Who's Who?* about Jesus of Nazareth. What would you write about him?

▶ What is significant about the two last lines of this poem? How are they linked to the rest of the poem?

The Craftsman

In the beginning
He just stayed close to his father,
Then his father taught him the names
Of all the tools –
Then he showed him how to hold them.
Then later as he grew stronger
He showed him how to use the different tools.
Soon he was able to earn a living.
His work varied from mending broken slats on donkey
    carts to fixing shelves and doors.

His mind went back
Over the last ten years or so.
And he remembered with a craftsman's pride,
The many boats he had repaired.
And how his work would continue to give good value
For many years to come.
He knew that some fishermen and boat-owners
Had received a bargain with his work.
For himself, he was grateful to have always given good
    value.
He thought too, of the great heavy haulks of timber
    and planking
That he carried on various jobs.
Sometimes he had wondered if the very sinews
In his arms would snap.
But somehow, praise God, he had always
Managed to complete his task.
Now all that was finished.
All that remained, was to carry this cross
To Golgotha, the Place of the Skulls.

(Bill Jones in *Liturgy of Life*, 1991)

11

5 CREEDS

If you ask Christians what they believe in, they will give you a series of statements which form a '**creed**'. The Latin word *credo* means 'I believe'.

The creeds used by Christians are centred on the person of Jesus Christ. They are made up of a number of statements telling you what Christians believe about Jesus and his relationship to the God whom he called 'Father'.

Christians see Jesus' relationship to God as unique. They claim that Jesus brings them to God in a way no one else does and that is why they call themselves followers of Jesus, not of someone else.

But how can Christians express that special relationship? What does it mean to say Jesus comes from God? Does it mean he comes from outside the human race, rather than from within? Does it mean he has powers quite different from other human beings? Does he have a divine nature as well as a human nature?

Throughout history, the leaders of the Christian communities (the bishops) have called meetings (councils) to discuss such questions and to agree an answer. They have needed to decide exactly what Christians believe, and to say that anything beyond this is 'heresy', that is, error, no longer the truth.

The earliest creed still used by Catholics is known as the *Apostles' Creed* because at one time it was thought to have been put together by the original twelve **apostles**, those chosen by Jesus as his closest companions. In fact, it comes from about 100 years later, when it was used as a statement of belief made by those being baptized.

The Apostles' Creed

I believe in God,
the Father almighty,
creator of heaven and earth,
and in Jesus Christ,
his only Son, Our Lord,
who was conceived by the Holy Spirit,
born of the Virgin Mary,
suffered under Pontius Pilate,
was crucified, died and was buried.
He descended into hell.
The third day he rose again from the dead.
He ascended into heaven
and is seated at the right hand of God
the Almighty Father.
From thence he shall come to judge
the living and the dead.
I believe in the Holy Spirit,
the Holy Catholic Church,
the Communion of Saints,
the forgiveness of sins,
the resurrection of the body,
and life everlasting. Amen.

REFLECTION

May your creed be for you as a mirror.
Look at yourself in it, to see if you believe
everything you say you believe.
And rejoice in your faith each day.

(St Augustine, quoted in
Catechism of the Catholic Church, 1994)

'May your creed be for you as a mirror'

Turn back to the tree diagram on p. 8. Notice the stumps of the two branches cut off in AD 325 and AD 450. They represent the heresies of the priest Arius (condemned at Nicea for denying that Jesus is 'of the same substance as God the Father') and of the bishop Nestorius (condemned at Chalcedon for denying that Jesus had a divine nature). Catholics still say or sing the *Nicene Creed* (formulated against Arius at Nicea in AD 325) every Sunday at Mass.

The Nicene Creed

We believe in one God,
the Father, the Almighty,
maker of heaven and earth,
of all that is, seen and unseen.

We believe in one Lord, Jesus Christ,
the only Son of God,
eternally begotten of the Father,
God from God, Light from Light,
true God from true God,
begotten, not made,
of one Being with the Father.
Through him all things were made.
For us men and for our salvation
he came down from heaven:
by the power of the Holy Spirit
he became incarnate from the Virgin Mary,
*   and was made man.*

For our sake he was crucified under Pontius Pilate;
he suffered death and was buried.
On the third day he rose again
in accordance with the Scriptures;
he ascended into heaven
and is seated at the right hand of the Father.
He will come again in glory
*   to judge the living and the dead,*
and his kingdom will have no end.

We believe in the Holy Spirit, the Lord,
*   the giver of life,*
who proceeds from the Father and the Son.
With the Father and the Son
*   he is worshipped and glorified.*
He has spoken through the Prophets.
We believe in one holy catholic and apostolic Church.
We acknowledge one baptism for the forgiveness of sins.
We look for the resurrection of the dead,
and the life of the world to come. Amen.

REFLECTION

'I believe' (Apostles' Creed) is the faith of the Church professed personally by each believer, principally during Baptism. 'We believe' (Nicene Creed) is the faith of the Church confessed by the bishops assembled in council or more generally by the liturgical assembly of believers. 'I believe' is also the Church, or mother, responding to God by faith as she teaches us to say both 'I believe' and 'We believe'.

(*Catechism of the Catholic Church*, No. 167)

THINGS TO DO

▶ What is a creed?

▶ Who were Arius and Nestorius?

▶ On a large sheet of paper, write the *Apostles' Creed* and the *Nicene Creed* side by side, in such a way as to compare them. How are they similar? How are they different?

And the Word became flesh and dwelt among us.

John 1:14

The word **incarnation** means 'in the flesh and blood'. Christians use the word to express their belief that God was present in the flesh and blood of the human Jesus.

Every Catholic first school and primary school is almost certain to spend December preparing a nativity play. Perhaps you have a photo at home of yourself as a shepherd with a tea-towel on your head, or as an angel with wings and a halo made from a wire coat hanger. The stories of Jesus' birth, originally told by Luke and Matthew, are retold year by year, century by century. The two stories are very different. Read *Luke*, chapters 1 and 2 and *Matthew*, chapters 1 and 2.

Luke's story about shepherds is a good introduction to his Gospel. Shepherds were considered outcasts from strict Judaism, and Luke's Gospel highlights God's preference for outcasts, sinners and minority groups.

Matthew's story about wise men from the East is a good introduction to his Gospel. His birth story is rooted in reference to Old Testament events and images, and Matthew's Gospel was written to convince the Jews that Jesus fulfilled all their hopes, as expressed in the Old Testament writings.

What can this simple piece of Gospel study tell us about the birth of Jesus? Did the writers have special information? Would a camcorder have been able to catch the nativity pictures? Were the skies really filled with singing angels? Did people truly understand who Jesus was as early as this?

Until recently, everyone assumed that these stories were as historical as the rest of the Gospel. When 'God becomes man' you expect strange things to happen. More recently, Bible scholars, both Catholic and Protestant, have shown that the nativity stories were later additions to the Gospel writings about Jesus' life, death and resurrection. They were not meant to be historical details, but poetic stories which expressed the writer's belief that in the history of the world, this birth was unique. Catholics are invited to ask the question 'What do the stories mean?', not 'What really happened?'

The school nativity play

QUESTIONS PEOPLE ASK

Some people ask 'What does it really mean that "The Word was made flesh and dwelt amongst us"?' It is easier, however, to say what it does not mean. The writers of the *Catechism of the Catholic Church* explained it this way:

> *The unique and altogether singular event of the Incarnation of the Son of God does not mean that Jesus Christ is part man, nor does it imply that he is the result of a confused mixture of the divine and the human. He became truly man while remaining truly God. Jesus Christ is true God and true man.*

(*Catechism of the Catholic Church*, No. 464)

The **Incarnation** is a mystery which cannot be fully understood. Sometimes believers catch a glimpse or insight into the meaning of the mysteries of their faith. A Catholic mother wrote the following reflection on the Incarnation, describing how she came to understand it.

Low in Marks

I never thought that kneeling on the floor of Marks and Spencer could give me a deep insight. But today it did.

I was on the floor measuring up a pair of trousers on Peter, when I suddenly saw, more clearly than ever before, the world as he sees it. It was most uncomfortable at that moment. Sales shoppers don't stop for little boys. Swinging shoulder bags missed our ears by inches. Bulging shopping baskets didn't. But worst of all was the mass of legs and arms, with hardly any faces, that pressed in upon us with claustrophobic effect.

No wonder the children complain about shopping. It isn't so much that they can't reach the counters to see what I'm looking at, it is this awful feeling of being beneath the adults, of being lowly and disadvantaged. Height gives power, I thought to myself as I paid for the trousers.

Rebecca was saying the other day that 'God is up in heaven'. This is a new language coming in from school. Peter is convinced God lives up in the moon. I wonder if this lofty height gives God more threatening power in their eyes. I hope it won't make him remote.

As every parent knows the happiest moments are often spent on the floor with the children. They love to climb on top of us to establish that they have power too.

As Rebecca knelt on my lap this evening, combing my hair – and my eyebrows – I thought how good it is that the Christian doctrine of Incarnation tells us to look for God here at eye-level, and not high up in the skies.

(Anon.)

'The Christian doctrine of Incarnation tells us to look for God here at eye-level, and not high up in the skies'

REFLECTION

A Catholic theologian writes:

> Jesus was everything that people had ever hoped and prayed for…
> He was in every way the ultimate…the only power which could transform the world.
> Jesus was experienced as the breakthrough in history.
> He transcended everything that had ever been said or done before.
> He was in every way the last word.
> He was on a par with God.
> His words were God's words. His Spirit was God's Spirit.
> His feelings were God's feelings.
> What he stood for was exactly the same as what God stood for.
> To believe in Jesus today is to agree in this assessment of him…
> To believe in Jesus is to believe that he is divine…
> To believe that Jesus is divine is to choose to make him and what he stands for your God.

(Albert Nolan OP, *Jesus Before Christianity*, 1976)

THINGS TO DO

▶ Write a brief summary of Luke's infancy story (*Luke* 1 and 2). Write a paragraph to show you have understood what Luke was *actually* telling his readers about Jesus.

▶ Write a brief summary of Matthew's infancy story (*Matthew* 1 and 2). Write a paragraph to show you have understood what Matthew was *actually* telling his readers about Jesus.

▶ What do you think Albert Nolan means by 'Jesus was experienced as the breakthrough in history'?

He suffered under Pontius Pilate,
was crucified, died and was buried.

(The Apostles' Creed)

People have been wearing crosses around their necks for centuries. Look at the photo of different crosses. You will probably recognize the fashionable ones sold in shops and markets today. But the large one is a silver and jewelled Crusader cross of the twelfth century. The small one, a fifth-century Byzantine cross, was dug up recently in Jerusalem. This cross was worn by a pilgrim visiting the Church of the Holy Sepulchre in Jerusalem, which marks the place where Jesus was executed on a cross and was buried.

Catholics recall Jesus' death every time they make the **sign of the cross** and every time they go to Mass (see p. 46). The cross badge has become the common symbol that unites all Christians.

Catholics continue to practise a form of prayer brought by the crusaders to Europe called the **Stations of the Cross**. They trace the footsteps of Jesus on his last journey through Jerusalem by meditating on the Gospel story. To help them do this pictures are placed around the church.

THE GOSPEL STORY

The Gospel writers were the first to put on record the whole story of Jesus' death. In fact, they wrote this part of the Jesus story first. Later they added long introductions to the **passion** (suffering) and death story. The events surrounding Jesus' death are commemorated for the whole week before Easter, known by Christians as **'Holy Week'**.

The Gospel story tells of Jesus' growing unpopularity with the Jewish religious authorities because his preaching was an embarrassment. It tells of his:

- anguished prayer in the Garden of Gethsemane
- betrayal by a close friend, Judas
- trial for blasphemy by the High Priest and his court
- trial for treason by the Roman Governor Pontius Pilate
- last journey through Jerusalem to execution hill, Calvary
- crucifixion (death on a cross) between two criminals
- burial by Joseph of Arimathea in a borrowed tomb.

A collection of crosses

QUESTIONS PEOPLE ASK

▶ Christians call the day that Jesus died Good Friday. What can be good about it? Death always brings sadness and pain. It is bad news. But Jesus' death was special because it showed he was willing to sacrifice his life for his friends. He died because he refused to change his teaching that God is Love. This is good news.

▶ 'Jesus died to save us from sin.' What does this mean?
Christians have always called the death of Jesus their salvation. Over the centuries attempts have been made to put this belief into clear words. Many of the images used in the past depended upon legal, secular language. They spoke of a judgemental God demanding the death of Jesus as satisfaction for sin; or of a lamb offered in sacrifice; or of a price paid to redeem people from slavery; or of a business transaction between two alienated parties (atonement). The **New Catechism** continues to use these traditional images. But there are other images which can be used to speak of the same underlying reality. Many Catholics today would say 'We are saved by Jesus because he gave us a new understanding of God. I look at the cross and I see what God is like – loving, forgiving, compassionate. I need to build my life on this model.' Many find this image closer to the language of the Gospel.

REFLECTIONS

Faithful Cross! above all other
One and only noble tree!
None in foliage, none in blossom,
None in fruit thy peer may be;
Dearest wood and dearest iron!
Dearest weight is hung on thee.

(From the Good Friday Liturgy,
Venantius Fortunatus, AD 530–609)

We adore you, O Christ, and we bless you.
Because by your holy Cross you have
redeemed the world.

(From the prayers of the *Stations of the Cross*)

A cross from El Salvador

THINGS TO DO

▶ Look at the photograph of the cross and the words of Father D'Escoto, below. Both come from Central America where following the Gospel can mean more than just wearing a cross (see p. 16) (Mark told the early Christians they had to be prepared to die for their faith.)

'I don't think we Christians have understood what carrying the cross means. We are not carrying the cross when we are poor or sick or suffering small everyday things – these are all part of life. The cross comes when we try to change things. That is how it came for Jesus.'

(Father M D'Escoto, Nicaragua)

What do you think Father D'Escoto would like to see changed in the world today?
The cross is from El Salvador. The figure is a leader of a local community. Some leaders have been killed for seeking justice for the poor.

▶ Design your own cross based on an issue that you think is important today.

▶ Find out about one of the following:

1 The Stations of the Cross
2 The difference between the four Gospel accounts of Jesus' death
3 How artists represent the crucifixion of Jesus (the art department may help you with pictures)
4 The **liturgy** (church service) of Good Friday

Present your work to the class.

If Christ has not been raised, then your faith is a delusion.

(Paul to the Corinthians, *1 Corinthians 15:17*)

When Catholics celebrate the **Resurrection** of Jesus on Easter night they call it 'Most Blessed of all nights'. The Resurrection is the central mystery of Christian faith. It is the 'night of the Passover when Christ passed from death to life and is the most important moment in the entire Christian Year'. (Pope John Missal, p. 335). Without it, the rest of the year would be meaningless.

Jesus died the ugly death of a criminal. But Christians believe that something extraordinary happened shortly afterwards. The disillusioned and dejected disciples suddenly became very excited and full of enthusiasm. They found the courage to preach the Good News of Jesus – of which they had despaired the day before. What had happened?

All four Gospel writers include an account of an empty tomb. But the stories do not agree on details.

WHAT DOES RESURRECTION MEAN?

Three Catholics were asked this question and here are their replies:

'Jesus died and was buried. His corpse was revived by God and the apostles saw him as clearly as I can see you. It was the greatest miracle ever.'

(Bob)

'The resurrection means new life. Jesus died but lives on in Spirit in the community. He lives on when people behave like him.'

(Anne)

'I never think of resurrection in the past. I think of wonderful ways today when life comes out of death. Look at people's generosity when there is a natural disaster.'

(Francis)

So Bob believes in an actual physical bringing back to life of Jesus' dead body. For centuries, most Catholics have taken the Easter story at face value like this, presuming that the texts record historical fact. But alongside, they have always spoken as Anne does, about Jesus living on in the community of believers – the Church.

Francis is more typical of those Catholics who ask questions about their faith and who are more interested in what resurrection means today, than in what actually happened at the tomb. He finds interesting what modern biblical scholars – both Catholic and Protestant – have to say: 'The empty tomb and the physical presence of Jesus could not have been filmed because the stories are not about that kind of reality'.

THINGS TO DO

▶ Read the four accounts of the empty tomb. You will find them in *Mark 16:1–8, Matthew 28:1–8, Luke 24:1–12, John 20:1–10*.

▶ Compare the stories:

1 What are the names of the women at the tomb?
2 Who were the messengers?
3 Are there any other differences?

Write out your answers in four columns, side by side.

Life can come out of death

WHAT KIND OF REALITY IS THE RESURRECTION?

Scholars point to the earliest mention of resurrection by Paul (*see 1 Corinthians 15:3–8*). Paul speaks of resurrection without mentioning any empty tomb. Was the 'empty tomb' simply the **evangelists'** (Gospel writers) dramatic way of saying that Jesus is not to be found in a graveyard; he lives on in a mysterious but real way, embodied in his disciples? In other words, the killing of Jesus did not put a stop to him. It made him live more powerfully than ever.

Many Catholics, such as Francis above, look at the situation in El Salvador, Central America, today and see that resurrection is a reality. The courage of Catholics there, in the face of deep suffering, is like new life springing up in a desert. These Christians are filled with courage and generosity by following the Gospel and living as Jesus did. In fact, Francis was simply echoing the words of the martyred Archbishop of San Salvador, Oscar Romero, who spoke of his own 'resurrection' in the lives of his people.

'I have often been threatened with death. Nevertheless, as a Christian, I do not believe in death without resurrection. If they kill me I will rise in the Salvadorian people.'

(Oscar Romero)

The official documents of the Catholic church continue to emphasize that the resurrection of Jesus was a historical event, not merely a spiritual experience in the heart of his followers.

THINGS TO DO

▶ Find out about the life and death of Oscar Romero. Write 150 words about him.

▶ Find out about the political/social situation of El Salvador. Write 150 words about it.

▶ In what ways do you think Romero has lived on in his people? Give examples of how you see Jesus living on in people today.

▶ Which of the explanations of the resurrection given by Bob, Anne and Francis makes the most sense to you? Explain why.

Archbishop Oscar Romero

9 THE HOLY SPIRIT

*We believe in the **Holy Spirit**, the Lord, the giver of life.*

(The Creed)

Catholics, like all Christians, speak of God in symbols, images and stories. It is the only way the human mind can approach the mystery of God.

One of the symbols used is that of 'Spirit' which means wind (and therefore, force or power), and breath (and therefore, life). When the Bible wants to describe how God relates to humans, it speaks of God's Spirit. The *Genesis* creation story begins with God bringing life out of nothing by breathing his Spirit over the waters of darkness. A later writer says:

The Spirit of the Lord fills the whole world.
It holds all things together
And knows every word spoken to man.

(Wisdom 1:17)

God is power. God is life. God is Spirit. The famous five New Testament writers used the same symbol to describe God's love and power. For example, Paul wrote:

The love of God has been poured into our hearts by his Spirit, who is God's gift to us.

(Romans 5:5)

Later in the same letter he wrote:

If the Spirit of God, who raised Jesus from death lives in you
then he who raised Christ from death will also give life to your mortal bodies by the presence of his Spirit in you.

(Romans 8:11)

Catholics celebrate this presence of God's Spirit at **baptism** (see Unit 15) where they open themselves to God in the way Jesus did:

As soon as Jesus came up out of the water he saw the heavens opening and the Spirit coming down on him like a dove.

(Mark 1:10)

Baptism is confirmed in the **sacrament** of **confirmation** (see Unit 16), where the coming of God's Spirit is again celebrated, in memory of Luke's story of the earliest experience of the Church:

Suddenly there was a noise from the sky which sounded like a strong wind blowing, and it filled the whole house where they were sitting. Then

'Spirit of Jesus, fire of Whitsun'

they saw what looked like tongues of fire which spread out and touched each person there. They were all filled with the Holy Spirit.

(Acts 2:1–4)

This happened on the Day of **Pentecost**. Catholics call this day *'Whit Sunday'* from the white clothes worn by people being baptized on that day.

The first Christians experienced Jesus as being so obviously full of this Spirit of God, that they easily spoke of the Spirit of Jesus, or the Spirit of Christ. They believed it was this Spirit which 'came down upon' them after he had died, not as something substituting for an absent Jesus, but as a new personal way in which he was present among his

'Spirit of Jesus, living water'

followers. Those who live as Jesus did, filled with his Spirit, believe that he is still with them.

The following poem by Peter De Rosa gathers together all the symbols Christians use to describe the power of God's love and creation.

Come Holy Spirit

v1. *Spirit of Jesus, living Water,*
In our dry hearts, a secret spring.
We'll never thirst but drink for ever from you
Deep within.

v2. *Spirit of Jesus, Wind from heaven,*
Where you come from we can't see.
But like the wind that blows upon the waters
We are free.

v3. *Spirit of Jesus, Fire of Whitsun,*
We so need your light and love.
Send us one parted tongue of your own fire
From above.

v4. *Spirit of Jesus, God's Anointing,*
Make us holy, make us strong.
Next to the cross of Christ our Saviour is where
We belong.

v5. *Spirit of Jesus, our Consoler,*
Take away our hearts of stone.
Give us a peace surpassing everything
The world has known.

v6. *Spirit of Jesus, First fruits in us*
Of the Glory God will give,
One day on our dry bones your Breath will come
And they shall live.

(Peter De Rosa, *Come Holy Spirit*, 1975)

THINGS TO DO

▶ As a class divide into six groups. Each group should produce a poster based on the six verses of Peter De Rosa's poem. To help you research the meaning of the symbols in each of the verses look at the following passages in the Bible:

v1. *Genesis 1:1–2, Psalm 42(41):1–2, John 4:1–15.*
v2. *Genesis 1:1–2 and 8:1, Exodus 15:8, Psalm 104(103):3–4, Acts 2:1–4.*
v3. *Exodus 3:1–6 and 19:16–18, Isaiah 66:15–16, Acts 2:1–4.*
v4. *Psalms 133(132):1–2, Isaiah 61:1–3, Luke 4:18, Hebrews 1:9.*
v5. *Deuteronomy 4:29, Jeremiah 31:20, Ezekiel 36:26, John 20:22–3.*
v6. *I Corinthians 15:20,23, Romans 8:18–23, Ezekiel 37, John 11:25.*

Note: the Psalm numbers in parentheses refer to the Douay Bible, which numbers most of the Psalms one behind the standard versions.

▶ Display the posters. Each group should then describe their symbols to the other groups.

REFLECTIONS

Spirit of Jesus, Wind, Water, Fire, come!
Spirit of Jesus, God's Anointing, come!
Spirit of Jesus, our Consoler, come!
Spirit of Jesus, loving Heart of God, come!
Spirit of Jesus, Dove of divine peace, come!
Spirit of Jesus, First fruits of the Glory, come!
Spirit of Jesus, Breath of the world's
Resurrection, come!

(Peter De Rosa, *Come Holy Spirit*, 1975)

Prayer often used by Christians

Come, Holy Spirit, fill the hearts of your faithful, and enkindle in them the fire of your love.
Send forth your Spirit and they shall be created.
And you shall renew the face of the earth.
Let us pray. O God, who has taught the hearts of the faithful by the light of the Holy Spirit, grant that by the gift of the same Spirit we may be always truly wise and ever rejoice in his consolation. Through Christ Our Lord. Amen.

Both at the beginning of Mass and at the end, the priest addresses the congregation in a three-fold formula which refers not simply to 'God', but to 'Father, Son and Spirit'. These are the words he uses:

> 'In the name of the Father, and of the Son, and of the Holy Spirit.'

> 'May Almighty God bless you, the Father, the Son, and the Holy Spirit.'

The same happens half way through the Mass, where the creed, said or sung by the congregation, also comes in three parts:

> 'We believe in one God, the Father…
> We believe in one Lord, Jesus Christ…
> We believe in the Holy Spirit, the Lord, the giver of life.'

This Christian way of referring to God as 'Three persons' is called 'trinitarian language', meaning three-in-one. The language is not easily understood by non-Christians, who suspect that although Christians talk of one God, they really believe in three. But the language is also not easily understood by many Christians, who find it so confusing that they prefer not to be reminded of it.

'The Holy Trinity' by Botticelli

WHY USE TRINITARIAN LANGUAGE?

Christians believe in one God only. They took over from Jesus himself the uncompromising Jewish belief that 'The Lord our God is one God'. Christians believe in the one God whom Jesus called Father and taught his followers to do the same, saying 'Our Father'.

While this one God remains essentially a mystery (otherwise he would not be God), the followers of Jesus claim that in the life and teaching and death of Jesus they have come to know God as fully as he can be known. For them, Jesus is, as it were, a window into God. In Jesus, they say, God has 'come down' from heaven and lived with us. In him, the reality of God has 'come through'. To look at Jesus is to see God in human form (see *John 14:9*).

This experience did not end when Jesus died. His physical presence was no longer with his followers. But they were convinced that the godly Spirit, which had always inspired Jesus, lived on. To live as Jesus did, in his 'Spirit' as they say, was to discover Jesus still present with them.

WHAT TRINITY DOES NOT MEAN

- It does not mean blurring the oneness of God. Christians do not believe in a God different from the one worshipped by Jews and Muslims too.

- It does not mean that Jesus was not fully a human being. What was divine about him has to be found in his humanity, not outside it.

- It does not mean that the same thing can be both three and one at the same time; or that one God equals three Gods; or that three persons equal one person.

WHAT TRINITY DOES MEAN

- **Trinity** means that Jesus was so close to God that when his followers think of Jesus they find themselves thinking of God, and when they think of God they find themselves thinking of Jesus.

- For Christians, the word 'God' can no longer be used on its own. Since the time of Jesus it will always have overtones of the man in whose life that one God was embodied (incarnation); and of the Spirit of Christ under whose inspiration all Christians try to live.

REFLECTION

Father,
You sent your Word to bring us truth
and your Spirit to make us holy.
Through them we come to know the mystery
*   of your life.*
Help us to worship you, one God in three
*   Persons*
by proclaiming and living our faith in you.

(Opening prayer of the Mass, *Trinity Sunday*)

THINGS TO DO

▶ Look up the following Bible texts:

   Psalm 9:2
   John 17:21
   1 John 4:7
   Wisdom 1:7
   Romans 5:5
   Psalm 69(68):1–3

   Write them out.

▶ Choose pictures from magazines to
   illustrate the texts and make small
   posters. There is an example below.

Save me, O God!
I am sinking in deep mud,
And there is no solid ground;
I am out in deep water and the waves
*   are about to drown me.*
I am worn out from calling for help.

(Psalm 69(68):1–3)

Father you are the source of all holiness. Through the prayers and examples of your saints, lead us to live holy lives.

(Prayer of the Church)

WHAT IS A SAINT?

Saints are people who lived their lives in imitation of Jesus, and based their lives, as Jesus did, on the **Beatitudes** (blessings) spoken by Jesus and recorded by Matthew in the *Sermon on the Mount*.

> *Blessed are the poor in spirit: for theirs is the kingdom of heaven.*
> *Blessed are the meek: for they shall possess the land.*
> *Blessed are they that mourn: for they shall be comforted.*
> *Blessed are they that hunger and thirst after justice: for they shall have their fill.*
> *Blessed are the merciful: for they shall obtain mercy.*
> *Blessed are the clean of heart: for they shall see God.*
> *Blessed are the peacemakers: for they shall be called the children of God.*
> *Blessed are they that suffer persecution for justice's sake: for theirs is the kingdom of heaven.*
> *Blessed are you when they shall revile you, and persecute you, and speak all that is evil against you, untruly, for my sake.*
> *Be glad and rejoice for your reward is great in heaven.*

(*Matthew 5:3–12*, Douay Version)

Saints first became popular in the fourth century, when people began to flock to the burial places of Christians who had lived outstanding lives, especially if they had been martyred. Shrines were built on their graves, and the name 'saint' was given to them by popular acclamation.

Many legends grew up around these early saints and, in many cases, it is difficult now to uncover the truth about their life stories. The Church authorities eventually took over the role of proclaiming people saints, by a process called **canonization**. The first saint to be recognized officially in this way was St Ulric, when Pope John XV canonized him in AD 993.

By the Middle Ages the veneration (honour) of saints was the main characteristic of popular religion. Their **relics** (remains) became highly important, and so did pilgrimages to their shrines. There was a good deal of paganism and superstition in this devotion to saints. While the Church certainly made a clear distinction between worshipping God and honouring saints, it is likely that many ordinary people saw no difference between the two.

It is the confusion over worship that worried the Protestant reformers. From the fifteenth century they revolted against what they called the 'cult' of saints, believing that they were taking the place of God. Reformers often smashed statues and painted out church murals (wall paintings).

The Roman Catholic Church never gave up its devotion to saints, always claiming that the **communion of saints** is a powerful help for ordinary people to grow more Christ-like. One Catholic teacher wrote:

> *An old name for this family-dimension of the Church is the 'Communion of Saints'. It means that all Christians here on earth are united in communion with the Christians who have gone before us and who are now with God. They have passed on their faith, hope and love to us; and they are our models of the Christian life. They are still with us by their prayers. It is as if they are part of the one prayer-group we belong to. Close to God as they are, they do not forget us.*

(Damian Lundy, *To Grow in Christ*, 1980)

Saints were ordinary men, women and children. Their lives were certainly not perfect all the time. They struggled and failed very often. But through God's grace, they eventually reached holiness. This gives Catholics today hope and encouragement. The box opposite shows that a saint of a previous age can inspire Christian people today. It is the outline for a prayer service organized by Christian peace groups on the Feast of St Francis of Assisi.

SAINT: the word means a holy person. The word 'holy' has many shades of meaning.

- In Hebrew, it means 'different', 'other','extraordinary' in a rather frightening way.
- In Greek and Latin, it means 'consecrated', 'removed from common use'.
- In English, it is related to the words 'whole' 'hale' and 'healthy'.

ST FRANCIS' DAY, 4 October

The 'Prayer of St Francis of Assisi' and the song 'Make me a channel of your peace' are well known to Christian peacemakers. One might even think of St Francis as the patron saint of the peace movement.

St Francis of Assisi

Our Purpose
To sow love where there is hatred, forgiveness where there is hurt, hope where there is despair, and joy where there is sadness. To find inspiration in the example of Francis of Assisi.

A Form of Worship
1 Prayer of St Francis
2 Reading about St Francis
3 Meditation, silence
4 Bible reading
5 Other readings
6 Song
7 Exchanging the peace of Christ
8 Prayer, meditation

Notes
Francis of Assisi was concerned about poverty and injustice, and about the natural world, as well as about peace and reconciliation. Situations of natural beauty (such as a peace garden) could be a suitable venue for the service. A place where there is much poverty would be another natural setting.

Since Francis was a friar whose life was dedicated to simplicity, love, joy and penitence, his feast would be an appropriate time to collaborate with his twentieth-century followers, the Franciscans. Plan the service jointly with them, or invite someone to come and lead the meditations.

(Adapted from V Flessati, *Prayers for Peacemakers*, 1988)

REFLECTIONS

'Do not weep, for I shall be more useful to you after my death and I shall help you then more effectively than during my life.'

(St Dominic to his brothers, quoted in the *Catechism of the Catholic Church*)

'I want to spend my heaven in doing good on earth.'

(St Thérèse of Lisieux quoted in the *Catechism of the Catholic Church*)

The *Feast of All Saints* (those canonized and those not) is on 1 November.

THINGS TO DO

▶ What does the word 'saint' mean?

▶ What does the Church mean by the 'Communion of Saints'?

▶ What is canonization?

▶ What would make you say of someone 'That person is a saint!'?

Catholics, like all Christians, believe that death is the beginning of new life. People die, they believe, into the love of God. This does not mean that Catholics are comfortable with death and the suffering and loneliness it brings. They remember that Jesus himself cried out on the cross: 'My God, my God why did you abandon me?' (*Mark 15:34*).

Sheila Cassidy, who has worked for many years with the dying, wrote:

> *Perhaps it is the grief of parents, the anguish of widowers that is the worst part of death, for however much we believe that 'the souls of the virtuous are in the hands of God', and 'no torment shall ever touch them' the grief remains and our hearts are pierced by a sword that is turned again and again by each passing memory.*

(Sheila Cassidy, *Good Friday People*, 1991)

Catholics pray that those who have died will share the life of God (eternal life) in heaven, in the company of Jesus and the saints. This hope of eternal life for those who die is expressed in Psalm 23 (22) – often said or sung at Christian funerals.

The Powazki cemetery in Warsaw

Psalm 23(22)

The Lord's my shepherd, I'll not want.
He makes me down to lie
in pastures green. He leadeth me
the quiet waters by.

My soul he doth restore again,
and me to walk doth make
within the paths of righteousness,
e'en for his own name's sake.

Yea, though I walk in death's dark vale,
yet will I fear no ill.
For thou art with me, and thy rod
and staff me comfort still.

My table thou hast furnishèd
in presence of my foes,
my head thou dost with oil anoint,
and my cup overflows.

Goodness and mercy all my life
shall surely follow me.
And in God's house for evermore
my dwelling place shall be.

(From the *Scottish Psalter*, 1650)

QUESTIONS PEOPLE ASK

What is heaven?

Heaven is to see, face to face, the God, and the Christ, and the saints, and the loved ones, whose faces are now hidden from us. St Peter wrote:

> *We've not seen him yet we love him. We've not seen him, yet our joy is too deep for words; We've not seen him, yet in faith we hold him, the Christ who waits for us.*

(1 Peter 1:8)

St Paul wrote: 'Now we see in a mirror darkly, but then face to face.' (*I Cor 13:12*)

St John wrote: 'We are God's children now; we do not yet know what we shall be when we see him as he is.' (*1 John 3:12*)

St Thomas Aquinas wrote: 'God alone can satisfy all our longings.'

The Catechism says: 'Heaven is the ultimate end and fulfilment of the deepest human longings, the state of supreme, definitive happiness.'

What is hell?

Christians have always believed that people are free to choose to accept God or to reject him totally. The state of living for all eternity without God is called **hell**. It is often spoken of in terms of fire, darkness, devils and horror, to emphasize the frightening responsibility laid on the shoulders of each person. Yet it is not as if God 'sends' people there. The Catechism says: 'God predestines no one to go to hell… [in fact] the Church implores the mercy of God who does not want "any to perish, but all to come to repentance" (2 Peter 3:9)'. Hence Julian of Norwich, the medieval hermit and writer, believed no one would finally finish up there (in her visions, hell was empty), because everyone would be forgiven by a loving God.

What is purgatory?

During the Middle Ages the Catholic Church taught that before those who died reached heaven they had to be cleansed, painfully, of every **sin** committed in life. **Purgatory** was this half-way stop and people were afraid of it. They aimed to shorten their stay there by gaining indulgences (time reduced for good behaviour). It was the sixteenth-century reformer Luther who questioned this teaching. Today, Catholics are less familiar with talk of purgatory, as they are more aware of the theological problem of 'spending a long time' in a state where time has come to an end, and see the needed purgation or cleansing taking place in a different way.

Jesus, Jesus, Jesus, give me here my purgatory.

(An old Catholic prayer)

REFLECTIONS

Brothers and sisters, we want you to know the truth about those who have died, so that you will not be sad, as those who have no hope. We believe that Jesus died and rose again, and so we believe that God will take back with Jesus those who have died believing in him.

(1 Thessalonians 4:13–14)

Catholic prayer

Eternal rest give unto them, O Lord.
And let perpetual light shine upon them.
May they rest in peace. Amen.

The *Feast of All Souls* is celebrated on 2 November when Catholics pray for those who have died.

THINGS TO DO

▸ Explain why you think Psalm 23(22) is often read or sung at Christian funerals.

▸ Look through the *Book of Psalms* in the Bible and choose another psalm you think would also be appropriate for a funeral reading.

▸ Test your knowledge of this section by answering the following:
   1 Why are the creeds important to Christians?
   2 Outline the main beliefs concerning Jesus in the *Apostle's Creed*.
   3 Choose a belief in one of the creeds which some people today would find difficult to accept. Give reasons for your choice.

The word **sacrament** *actually means 'a signpost pointing to the Holy One'. Jesus was himself the sacrament of God*

A Catholic poet, Gerard Manley Hopkins, wrote a poem that begins with the lines:

The world is charged with the grandeur of God.
It will flame out, like shining from shook foil.

(Gerard Manley Hopkins, 'God's Grandeur')

It is not unlike the psalmist who wrote, hundreds of years earlier:

The heavens declare the glory of God.

Not everybody would agree. Some people will look into the skies and see only threatening rain clouds and feel angry at the probability of no play in the cricket test match at Headingley.

The two poets here were men of faith, and they looked through the finite into the infinite; through what religious people call the secular to the sacred.

The world is charged with the grandeur of God

Poets and people of faith use a language of 'symbol' to express what they see with insight rather than with ordinary sight. One man, saddened at the loss of religious faith in the Western world has written:

The disease of the Western world is an eye-disease, an astigmatism which has narrowed vision so that men only see things as surface.

(Hugh Lavery, *Sacraments*, 1982)

God is a mystery beyond all mysteries. But Catholics, like all religious people, try to find words and ideas that will express something of that mystery. They look for symbols and signs that they can touch, to remind them of the God who cannot be touched. The poets saw creation itself as such a symbol. Other believers use holy statues, holy pictures, holy buildings, holy people, holy stories or holy ceremonies to keep them in touch with the mystery they call God.

Catholics call these signs or symbols of God **sacraments**.

The word actually means 'a signpost pointing to the Holy One'. When a sacrament points to God, the Holy One, it actually makes it possible for people to get closer to God.

Catholics understand sacraments best when they realize that Jesus was himself the sacrament of God. He made God real and close to people. Jesus is the signpost to God.

Catholics have seven special ways of celebrating the good news that the life and death of Jesus brought God close to them. They call these the seven sacraments of the Church:

- the Eucharist
- Baptism
- Confirmation
- Reconciliation
- Marriage
- Orders
- Anointing the sick

Units 14–20 look at each of these in detail.

Catholics believe, with other Christians, that Jesus made God real to people in a number of ways:

- by his concern for the sick and the poor
- by his teaching, so full of compassion
- by his own living out of that teaching
- by his death on the cross where he forgave those who killed him.

It was his dignified acceptance of death that Jesus' friends could not forget. They recalled it by doing what Jesus had told them to do in remembrance of him, on the night before he died. They broke bread and poured wine to re-present (to make present again) the body that was broken and the life-blood of Jesus that was poured out.

This memorial celebration is called the **Eucharist**. Eucharist means thanksgiving. Christians who celebrate the Eucharist do so in different ways, though the heart of the service always remains the same. Roman Catholics call it the Mass. The leader of the community gives thanks to God and blesses the bread and wine, repeating the words of Jesus:

'Take this, all of you, and eat it:
this is my body which will be given up for you…

Take this, all of you, and drink from it:
this is the cup of my blood,
the blood of the new and everlasting covenant.
It will be shed for you and for all men
so that sins may be forgiven.
Do this in memory of me.'

The photo below shows a Catholic First Communion service. The whole parish shares in a celebration when children, usually aged about seven, receive the Eucharist for the first time.

The illustration on page 31 shows the rich symbolism of the sacrament of Eucharist. It is based on a poster used in many Catholic parishes today to instruct people becoming new members of the Church. It shows three aspects of the sacrament.

SACRIFICE

On the left of the illustration, in the shadow of the cross, are wheat and grapes. Both are grown from seeds that have to die in the ground before they can give new life. The community of believers is also in its shadow. The wheat is ground into the bread. The grapes are crushed into the wine.

Children receive their First Communion at St Mary of the Angels, London

THANKSGIVING

In the centre of the illustration, the community gathers together with the scriptures open and the bread and wine ready to be transformed into the Body and Blood of the Lord. Everyone is united by Christ's presence for he said, 'Where two or three are gathered together in my name, I will be in the midst of them.'

MINISTRY

On the right of the illustration, the community leaves the table to act as Jesus did – serving others, especially the poor and the hungry. That this is the meaning of the Eucharist is made clear by John, the last of the Gospel writers. He makes no mention of the bread and wine at the last supper meal. Instead, he gives great importance to the washing of the disciples' feet, as if it was this action that Jesus told his friends to do, in his memory:

'I have set an example for you, so that you will do just what I have done for you.'

(John 13:15)

The symbolism of the sacrament of Eucharist

Sharing some rice

THINGS TO DO

▶ The following are scripture passages that refer to the three parts of the illustration on this page.

1 Sacrifice: *Exodus 13:3–10; 1 Corinthians 11:23–25; John 12:23–5*
2 Thanksgiving: *John 6:35; Luke 14:15; Matthew 26:26–7; Acts 2:42; Deuteronomy 8:3*
3 Ministry: *John 13:1–15; Ephesians 3:17–19; Acts 2:44–5*

Read each passage in turn and show how each one is related to the sacrament of Eucharist.

▶ Read the reflection. In what way is this story related to the Eucharist?

REFLECTION

Some weeks back I heard there was a family that had not eaten for some days – a Hindu family – so I took some rice and I went to the family. Before I knew where I was, the mother of the family had divided the rice into two and she took the other half to the next door neighbours, who happened to be a Muslim family. Then I asked her: 'How much will all of you have to share? There are ten of you with that bit of rice.' The mother replied: 'They have not eaten either.' This is greatness.

(Mother Teresa of Calcutta, *A Gift from God*, 1975)

Catholics dip their hand into a water-stoup as they enter a church and make the sign of the cross on themselves. They do this to be reminded of their baptism. Water is the symbol of baptism. Christians think how Jesus 'drowned' in suffering and death, and rose again into new life. 'Baptism' means being immersed in water, as Jesus was immersed in death. It is the first sacrament Christians receive, their initiation or entry into the Christian community.

Christians believe that by this ceremony their past life is, as it were, washed away, and that they now stand before God in utter newness, like Christ himself, risen from the dead. Some Christian denominations, like Baptists, baptize adults only. The Catholic Church baptizes infants so that families can celebrate the birth of a new baby and the Church community can welcome the new member into its family. Parents and specially chosen godparents profess their belief in the teachings of the Church on the baby's behalf.

Baby Bridget is clothed in the new white garment of baptism

WATER AS A SYMBOL

Water is a very powerful symbol. Water gives life, but can also bring death. Flood waters bring devastation; heavy rains can destroy crops; rough seas can cost lives.

But water revives exhausted athletes; showers refresh hot bodies; rain brings back life to wilting plants. So water represents death and life. In baptism, believers share the death of Jesus in order to rise again with him to new life.

By our Baptism, then, we were buried with him and shared his death, in order that, just as Christ was raised from death by the glorious power of the Father so also we might live a new life.

(*Romans 6:4*)

THE BAPTISM CEREMONY

1 The parents and godparents profess their belief by reciting the creed on the baby's behalf.
2 The priest says a prayer of exorcism, asking that the baby may be rescued from the Slavery of Sin, and pass into the Freedom of God.
3 The baby is anointed with oil, like a fighter preparing for battle.
4 Water is poured over the baby's head as the priest says: '(Name…) I baptize you in the name of the Father and of the Son and of the Holy Spirit. Amen.'
5 The baby is dressed in a white garment as a sign of sharing the resurrection of Christ.
6 A candle is lit from the Easter candle which represents the risen Christ. It is given to a godparent on behalf of the baby as a sign of sharing the new life of Christ.

A Catholic baptism in Japan

'My parish of Musashigaoka stands on the edge of Kumamoto City, a new community. When our leaders were making plans for celebrating Easter we felt open to new ideas. Easter is the time when new members join the community. Back home we rarely get a chance to witness adult baptism. It is a great experience.

We wondered at our meeting if there wasn't another way of going about our baptism ceremony. Complete immersion was the common practice in the early Church…So we thought we would give it a try. Some people were shocked and there were many jokes. But we now have our new Baptistry, a big, beautifully tiled pool in the floor, right in the middle of our chapel.

Long ago when the Israelites were in Egypt they were slaves. In passing through the waters of the sea they left slavery behind and came out on the far side as free people. In the same way the newly baptized are seen journeying through water from slavery to freedom. Instead of a few drops of water being poured over their heads, our catechumens are totally immersed. It is amazing how this highlights the meaning of baptism, how they are now being buried with Christ and dying to everything that makes them less alive, less human, so they can rise to new life again in Christ.

Just before entering the water, the catechumens (candidates for baptism) remove the robe they have been wearing. They are putting off the old dark self, and when they emerge from the water they are presented with the 'white garment'. In baptism they have put on Christ. They are a new creation.

On that first Holy Saturday night the pool became a focus of attention with lights shining on the water and candles held above. There were eight people waiting to be baptized. Not unnaturally they were feeling tense…When the actual moment of baptism came the atmosphere changed. We were carried along by a powerful and moving drama. It was beautiful. One by one the eight were escorted to the water by godparents, descended the steps and were gently immersed. White garments were presented and they were led from the pool to the presbytery to change into the dry clothes. I had to change too. As we did so the baptistry was transformed into an altar. I will never forget the sight that awaited me as I joined the others. The newly baptized were waiting in long white garments to process back into the church. They were aglow. We all renewed our baptismal vows and I invited the non-Christian relatives and friends to share in a washing of hands as a sign that we all wanted to live in service of others.'

(Father Harry O'Carroll, Columban missionary)

Father Harry O'Carroll baptizes adults in his Japanese parish

THINGS TO DO

▶ Explain the use of the symbols, water and a candle, in the Catholic baptism service.

▶ What is the role of a godparent in the baptism ceremony?

▶ Do you think the complete immersion form of baptism is a good idea? Give reasons for your answer.

Most Catholics are baptized as babies long before they can understand what it means to be a disciple of Jesus. Their parents have promised to bring them up to live as generously as Jesus did. But when they are old enough to understand how difficult this can be, they are invited to confirm their baptism – **confirmation**. They are asked to make those early promises their own.

In many places nowadays, this commitment to Christ is made by Catholics when they are about 14 years old. Here is how two sisters see the importance of this sacrament in their faith journey. They were confirmed on Pentecost Sunday, the most appropriate day for the celebration.

Joanna and Katy wearing their confirmation T-shirts

'I decided to have my confirmation because I wanted to confirm what had been said for me at baptism. Until my confirmation, everything had been decided for me and then it was up to me. After my confirmation, I seemed different. I had a new courage and understanding of things. The preparation was done in a group and led by the school chaplain, Fr Dick. I enjoyed it thoroughly and seemed to get closer to the people in the group, which included my sister. For our preparation, we were not preached at, we did different things each week that helped us to understand the meaning and commitment of confirmation. I liked the way in which it was done because it was interesting and not just words and rules from a book. One of the practical things we did was to design and print our own T-shirt, with the design based on the symbols for the Spirit of God.'

(Joanna Carr, aged 14)

'Instead of taking my confirmation with the rest of my class when I was twelve, I decided to wait. I wanted it to really mean something – instead of just being as a matter of course. Even as I started the sessions, I was not sure of my decision. This was a big thing for me as it meant I had to take responsibility for being a Christian. Taking responsibility is not one of my strong points, and I was far from convinced of my views on certain aspects of the Church. However, as the weeks progressed, my fears subsided. I realized that taking a larger role in the Church did not have to mean agreeing blindly, under oath. What

particularly struck me was a talk given by the St Vincent de Paul group. To me, their ethos encapsulates everything a confirmed member of Church should be. Blindly generous, active and always positive. There can be no conflict in electing to try to live like this.'

(Katy Carr, aged 17)

Joanna and Katy presented themselves to the bishop, who is the 'father' of the local community. He laid his hands on their heads as a sign that he was appointing them to a task, and prayed for them to receive the gifts of the Holy Spirit. On their foreheads he made the sign of the cross, with the holy chrism oil, a sign of strength and a reminder of their commitment to follow Christ even to the cross.

The bishop prayed in these words, describing the gifts of the Spirit first mentioned by the Prophet Isaiah:

Send your Holy Spirit upon them to be their helper and their guide.
Give them the spirit of wisdom and understanding, the spirit of right judgement and courage, the spirit of knowledge and reverence.
Fill them with the spirit of wonder and awe in your presence.

REFLECTIONS

In baptism we are born to new life, after baptism we are confirmed for combat. In baptism we are washed, after baptism we are strengthened.

(Faustus of Riez, AD 460)

The authentic Christian faith which we profess has to be lived with enthusiasm. Enthusiasm is a flame which so many contrary winds today try to extinguish. Where is the enthusiasm of our faith today? There are no doubt many living members of the Church – a great many – who live and feel this joyous and generous enthusiasm. To these brothers and sisters, let us now give our greeting and blessing, like a breath of Pentecost.

(Pope Paul VI)

For wherever they live, all Christians are bound to show forth, by the example of their lives and by the witness of their speech, that new man which they put on at baptism, and that power of the Holy Spirit by which they were strengthened at Confirmation. Thus other men, observing their good works, can glorify the Father and can better perceive the real meaning of human life and the bond which ties the whole community of mankind together.

(Second Vatican Council, *The Missions*)

The Spirit produces love, joy, peace, patience, kindness, goodness, faithfulness, humility and self-control... And those who belong to Christ Jesus have to put to death their human nature with all its passions and desires. The Spirit has given us life; he must also control our lives.

(Paul to the Galatians, 5:22–5)

THINGS TO DO

▶ Look at the list of Fruits of the Spirit (Paul to the Galatians 5:22–5)

  1 Choose one that you think describes someone you know, e.g. 'My mother has the gift of kindness because…'.

  2 Choose one that you think describes a group or organization, e.g. 'The Samaritans have the gift of patience because…'.

▶ Design a confirmation logo for a banner or a T-shirt.

▶ '15 years old is a good age for confirmation.' Why would this be? Write about 200 words giving your view.

▶ Read carefully the statement made by the Second Vatican Council about confirmed Christians:

  1 What is the 'real meaning of human life' it mentions?

  2 From what you have read on these pages, give some examples of the qualities that could influence others and bring them 'to glorify the Father' (see also Unit 9).

Forgiveness of sin is one of the key Christian doctrines. Jesus preached the good news that God is always forgiving people, no matter what wrongs they commit. He treats good people and bad people in the same way. Roman Catholics celebrate this extraordinary generosity of God in the sacrament of **Reconciliation.**

King Hussein of Jordan being reconciled with Israel's leader Yitzhak Rabin after years of enmity

THE OLD FORM OF SACRAMENT (CONFESSION)

Many older Catholics remember being taken as children week after week to **confession**. It was a set routine. The penitents (sinners) went into a confessional box, a dark small room, and spoke anonymously to the priest hidden behind a screen. They gave a list of their sins and waited for a few words of encouragement from the priest. He then gave them a **penance** – usually prayers to say. They said an act of **contrition** (sorrow for sin) and the priest said words of **absolution** (forgiveness). Some Catholics are still helped by this pattern of confession, but it has declined dramatically as a way of celebrating God's forgiveness of sin.

Many reasons are suggested for the change in behaviour of Catholics:

- Some people, through lack of faith and prayer, are no longer aware of their sin, or feel a need for forgiveness.

- Others have rebelled against the low self-image and the threatening view of God encouraged by frequent confession.

- Many have grown uncertain about what is sinful and what is not, especially in matters of sex (e.g. contraception).

- More and more people feel that constant private confession encourages a sense of selfishness and that it does not cope with the far wider sinfulness of racism, exploitation of women and the poor, the arms race, etc.

One Catholic priest has summed it up like this:

> *The sacrament of confession, in the experience of many people, had belonged to a spirituality which reflected an obsession with sin and a sense of being overwhelmed with guilt. It encouraged within people a very poor self image, with little experience of forgiveness and that sense of being accepted.*

(Peter Wilkinson, *Focus on the Sacraments*, 1987)

THE NEW UNDERSTANDING OF THE SACRAMENT

Catholics today have not lost their sense of the sinfulness of themselves and of the world. They have returned to the Scriptures to find there the liberating news that God loves without measure and that, as the example of Jesus showed, he seeks out sinners to shower them with compassion. When Jesus was criticized for keeping the company of sinners and outcasts he replied: 'It is not the healthy who need the doctor, but the sick. I did not come to call the virtuous but sinners.'

One of the most powerful parables in the Gospels is the story of the Prodigal Son. Read the story in *Luke 15:11–32*. A teacher told this parable to her class and finished by saying: 'The boy's father said, "Welcome home, son. If you promise never to do it again, we will forget the past and put on a party…" The class said, "Hey, Miss, that wasn't in the story." What did they mean, do you think? Perhaps the following exercise will help you to see the point.

TEST YOURSELF

If you think about it, God could respond to sin in different ways:

- by exploding with anger: 'You have broken my commands – get out of my sight.'
- by a controlled rage: 'You have done me wrong. I demand you compensate to make it up to me.'
- by a generous forgiveness, with one condition: 'I love you, so I forgive you. Just promise, you won't sin again.'
- by a prodigal (over-generous) forgiveness. 'I love you. I've forgotten already what you did wrong. Come and be close to me.'

Which way does the Gospel see God? Which way do you see God? Are they the same?

THE SINFUL SITUATION OF THE WORLD

Over the past 30 years the Catholic Church has developed a new understanding of sin, stressing its communal nature. The older Church language spoke of **original sin** as a stain on the soul of individuals inherited at birth from Adam. Today, many Catholics consider original sin to be the sinful situation of the whole world into which we are born. Examples are in the news every day – the misery of Rwanda and Bosnia, the exploitation of the poor, and the greed power and money can bring.

Many young Catholics feel a responsibility for the world and have exchanged the tradition of personal confession for a commitment to the victims of the sinful world situation. The young people described in Unit 34 are good examples of this.

Church leaders are aware of this shift of emphasis. It was this that brought about a renewal of the sacrament, and a change of name from Penance to Reconciliation, at the the Second Vatican Council. In 1983 Pope John Paul II called a Synod of Bishops to discuss 'Reconciliation and Penance in the Mission of the Church'. Five days of discussion produced a balance between reflections on personal sin and 'social sin'. The English Archbishop Worlock

was one of those who asked for less emphasis on personal failings and more on social justice. 'The search for social justice', he said, 'could lead to a desire for reconciliation with God'.

REFLECTION

'I have been a school chaplain for two years now and the students are teaching me! I have discovered a new way of approaching the Sacrament of Reconciliation. Some classes prepare Services of Reconciliation, especially during Lent. Something new is happening. At first, as I expected, individuals would come afterwards for a private confession. This, after all, is what we encourage. But now groups of friends come together to talk over their problems, weaknesses and worries. They speak openly about their failings – in front of each other. In other words, they have rediscovered the need to confess sinfulness before the community. It is quite wonderful.'

(A high school chaplain)

THINGS TO DO

▶ Some elderly members of the parish are distressed that young people no longer go to confession. The priest has asked you to reassure them. Write a letter to the parish newsletter outlining your views. Make your letter positive.

▶ Rewrite the story of the Prodigal Son, putting it into a twentieth-century context. Show clearly what Luke was saying about forgiveness.

If God is love (St John's definition in his first letter, 4:16), then many people will be closest to God when they love one another. For very many people, loving relationships lead to **marriage.** Catholics, like all Christians, believe that the love husbands, wives, parents and children have for each other, is an image of God's love for everyone. Marriage is for Catholics, a sacrament, a signpost truly pointing to God.

It is Jesus who makes this clear. His followers recognize that the kind of love he showed on the cross not only demonstrated what God is like but was also a model for their own selfless love. Love always costs. Marriage therefore is demanding and not an easy way of life.

All Christian Churches teach that marriage is a serious and lifelong commitment. Roman Catholic couples usually exchange their marriage vows to one another in a religious service which becomes part of the Mass. It is then called a Nuptial Mass.

THE MARRIAGE SERVICE

- A greeting

The couple are welcomed by the priest and the community is asked to share in the joy of the celebration.

- The sermon

The priest outlines the meaning of a Christian marriage and the responsibilities it brings.

A Roman Catholic couple exchange their marriage vows during a religious service

- The marriage ceremony

This is in several parts:

a *The questions*

- Have you come to offer yourself to each other freely, without reservation?
- Will you honour and love each other for life?
- Will you accept children lovingly from God?

By answering the questions the couple publicly announce their readiness to take their responsibilities seriously.

b *The exchange of marriage vows*
The couple make vows to each other and in this way administer the sacrament to one another. The priest is there to witness it, and to represent the community of the Church. Each say in turn: 'I (name) do take thee (name) to be my lawful wedded wife/husband, to have and to hold from this day forward, for better, for worse, for richer, for poorer, in sickness and in health, to love and to cherish, till death do us part.'

The priest replies: 'You have declared your consent before the Church. May the Lord in his goodness strengthen your consent and fill you both with his blessings. What God has joined together let no man put asunder.'

c *The exchange of rings*
The ring, a sign of love and fidelity, is blessed and placed on the bride's finger by her partner, with the words: 'Take this ring as a sign of my love and fidelity in the name of the Father and of the Son and of the Holy Spirit.' If the husband wishes to wear a ring, that can also be blessed.

d *The marriage (nuptial) blessing*
Towards the end of the Mass the priest goes to the bride and prays for her in these words: 'Let us pray that God will bless this woman, give her love and peace. May her husband recognize that she is his equal and the heir with him to the life of grace. May he always honour her and love her as Christ loves his bride the Church. Keep them faithful to you and to each other and let them be living examples of Christian life.'

e *Signing the marriage register*
All Church marriages require civil recognition and for this the register must be signed before a registrar and witnesses.

THE MEANING OF THE SACRAMENT OF MARRIAGE FOR A CATHOLIC

- Marriage is a sign for all to see of God's faithful love.

- Marriage is an exclusive relationship (monogamy – one partner).

- Marriage is a lifelong relationship.

- Marriage is lifegiving, involving the acceptance of children as a gift from God.

A Catholic priest, Fr Peter Wilkinson, explains it in these words:

> *Marriage therefore, must first of all be lifegiving for husband and wife, whereby they make each other more fully human, more fully alive. It is in this lifegiving relationship that the image of God is to be found, in becoming one flesh. The husband is called to live for the wife, the wife for the husband.*
>
> (Peter Wilkinson, *Focus on the Sacraments*, 1987)

He then outlines the following qualities which such selfless commitment requires:

- A great act of faith to accept each other for better, for worse; constant communication which comes from respect for one another

- A listening to one another's needs and views

- A capacity for healing and forgiveness

- A joyful and fulfilling experience of human sexuality

- A responsible attitude to parenthood for 'indeed children are the supreme gift of marriage and greatly contribute to the good of parents themselves' (*Gaudium et Spes*, 50).

Parenthood is, for a Catholic believer, one of the most privileged ways human beings are called to imitate God in his creative work. Every baby should be wanted and cherished.

REFLECTIONS

How shall we ever be able adequately to describe the happiness of that marriage which the Church arranges, which the sacrifice strengthens, upon which the blessing sets a seal, at which the angels are present as witnesses, and to which the Father gives his consent.

(Tertullian, third century)

Not sex, but the ability to forgive one another is required premarital experience. In the words of St Paul: "Bear with one another; forgive each other as soon as a quarrel begins. The Lord has forgiven you; now you must do the same." (Colossians, 3:13)

(Peter Wilkinson, *Focus on the Sacraments*, 1987)

CLASS DEBATE

Read the reflection carefully. Hold a debate:

> This house believes Wilkinson is right: 'Not sex, but the ability to forgive one another is required premarital experience.'

Two people should propose the motion and two should oppose it.

THINGS TO DO

▶ Write a reply to an article in a magazine which claimed that marriage is old-fashioned and outdated. Your reply should be from a Christian point of view.

▶ What problems do you think could arise if a convinced Catholic wanted to marry a non-believer?

If one of you wants to be great, he must be the servant of the rest; and if one of you wants to be first, he must be the slave of all. For even the Son of Man did not come to be served; he came to serve and to give his life to redeem many people.

(*Mark 10:42–5*)

The martyred Archbishop Oscar Romero once said, 'Priests being killed is good news.' This is a strange thing to say, but he was responding to the fact that some of his priests were killed for serving the poor and challenging the authorities over the unjust treatment of people. As bishop he was glad that his priests were genuine followers of Jesus.

The New Testament tells Christians that by baptism all believers are called into one priesthood of Christ, and so are called to proclaim the Good News of Jesus Christ. St Peter wrote of this:

You are a chosen race, a royal priesthood, a consecrated nation, a people set apart to sing the praises of God.

(*Peter 2:9*)

This means that no one group of Jesus' followers can really claim to be 'in charge' of the Church, although a group can be 'charged' to serve it. All the community make up the Church. However, as the Christian community grew in numbers, it became essential, for the sake of good **order**, to appoint one person in each district to take parental care of the communities there.

In the first instance, these would be the Apostles whom Jesus had commissioned, under the leadership of Peter, to preach the Gospel to all people. They made further appointments of 'overseers' or bishops, and when the work increased others were called to help in instructing, baptizing, healing and preaching.

In the Acts of the Apostles the helpers were called 'elders' (*Acts 14:23*) and deacons, like Stephen (*Acts 6:8–10*) and Philip (*Acts 8:4–13*).

By the third century, the leadership of the communities had settled into a pattern.

- Lay people exercised many ministries themselves according to their gifts.

- Deacons were assistants to the bishop, especially in the liturgy.

- Presbyters shared the bishop's Eucharist and acted as a parish council.

- Bishops led local churches and their main task was preaching the Gospel and presiding at the Eucharist.

In later centuries, the role of bishops changed to administrators, and the presbyters became pastoral leaders of the local Church. The two offices became influential and important in the secular world, with bishops and clergy (presbyters) wearing special dress and being exempt from paying taxes or doing military service. A distinction between 'clergy' and 'laity' was firmly fixed. This was unfortunate because priests and bishops became almost exclusively associated with sacred rites and liturgical celebration, and they were presumed to have answers to all problems. The primary role as a follower of Jesus Christ – the servant of the poor – became lost. Lay people imagined that the Mass belonged to the clergy, and that they, the laity, were always in 'second place' before God.

THE ROMAN CATHOLIC CHURCH

Deeply aware of the rapid change in society, and of an educated Catholic laity who wanted more recognition in the twentieth-century Church, the Pope and bishops took a major step to remodel Church ministry. The new model was presented at the *Second Vatican Council* in the 1960s. Documents both on the laity and on priests restored the balance between the community of the Church. In an introduction to the Council document about priests, Bishop Guildford Young shows the change of view:

The idea of a priestly caste is excluded in the first chapter. The priest remains a 'disciple of the Lord'; he belongs to the People of God; he is to be a brother among brothers vis à vis *the laity. The priest has his special duties and his special sacramental grace, with a consequent definite quality of priestly holiness. But the virtues that are first listed to be his are significantly those of any authentic Christian: 'kindliness of heart, sincerity, strength of soul, constancy, assiduous regard for justice'. And a theme returning frequently is 'service'. Service of God and of the family of God.*

(*Documents of Vatican II, 1966*)

THE FUTURE OF THE CATHOLIC CHURCH

Since the fourth century, it has been a characteristic of the Catholic Church to have celibate (non-married) priests. It became Church law in AD 1139. There is also no ordained ministry for women. Following the recent review of the priest's role in the Church, it seems possible that the more fundamental questions about priesthood will be asked one day – is there a place for married priests (it would seem so, with a number of married Anglican priests joining the Catholic Church recently)? Some continue to ask if there is a place for women priests, too. The present pope has ruled this out of the question, though he continues to encourage women to be more actively involved in the Church's many ministries.

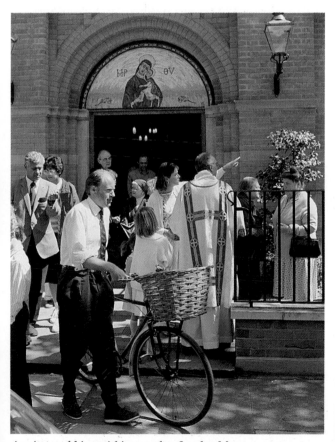

A priest and his parishioners after Sunday Mass

THINGS TO DO

 Write an article for a newspaper in response to this comment by a Catholic priest:

Women are playing an increasing role within the churches, which includes the role of priesthood. We need to listen to these various voices; they call for old wrongs to be redressed and for new forms of ministry and service to be made possible. It may be that only the full participation of women in the Church's ministry can really do justice to the compassion of Christ.

REFLECTIONS

The priesthood requires a great soul; for the priest has many harassing troubles of his own and has need of innumerable eyes on all sides.

(St John Chrysostom)

Every priest relies on the faith and talents of his parish community… The partnership between priests and people is built upon prayer, collaboration and mutual respect and love.

(Pope John Paul II at Heaton Park, 1982)

Is any man sick among you? Let him bring in the priests of the Church, and let them pray over him, anointing him with oil in the name of the Lord. And the prayer of faith shall save the rich man; and the Lord shall raise him up: and if he be in sins, they shall be forgiven him.

(James 5:14–15, Douay Version)

The Gospel is full of stories about Jesus healing the sick and comforting sinners. In fact, this is the most impressive part of his ministry, and the evidence he himself pointed to, to show that God's Kingdom was here and now – in this life – whenever such compassion was shown. In one incident, John the Baptist sent messengers from his prison to ask Jesus if he was the one whom people expected to bring the Kingdom. Jesus replied:

'Go back and tell John what you are hearing and seeing: the blind see, the lame walk, those who suffer from dreaded skin diseases are made clean, the deaf hear, the dead are brought back to life, and the Good News is preached to the poor. How happy are those who have no doubts about me.'

(Matthew 11:4–6)

It is hardly surprising, therefore, that Christians have always tried to imitate Jesus' care for the sick and the dying. By doing so they too are close to God himself.

Roman Catholics have a sacrament of **Anointing** the sick, remembering that Jesus was eager for his disciples to heal the sick as he did:

'And these signs shall follow them that believe…they shall lay their hands upon the sick, and they shall recover.'

(Mark 16:17–18)

HISTORY OF THE SACRAMENT

Until about AD 800, the people brought oil to their bishop, who blessed it for them to take home for family use.

For the next 300 years, until AD 1150, the priest took over the role of anointing the sick before they confessed their sins at the point of death.

From AD 1150–1550 it was the sacrament of dying and could only be received once.

After AD 1550 (Council of Trent) it was recognized that anointing could bring about bodily healing, but it was still known as the sacrament of **Extreme Unction** i.e. a consecration for death.

Caring for the sick

Vatican Council II and the New Rite of Pastoral Care of the Sick

At the Vatican Council in 1963, the sacrament was renamed 'Anointing the Sick'. Its primary purpose was specified as bringing comfort to sick people, helping them to trust in God and giving them strength to overcome their temptations to despair and their anxiety about death.

When the New Rite was introduced in 1983, it was made very clear that ministry to the sick is the responsibility of every Christian – as a follower of Jesus.

*This ministry is the common responsibility
of all Christians,
who should visit the sick,
remember them in prayer,
and celebrate the sacraments with them.
The family and friends of the sick,
doctors and others who care for them,
and priests with pastoral responsibilities
have a particular share
in the ministry of comfort.
Through words of encouragement and faith
they can help the sick
to unite themselves with the the sufferings
of Christ for the good of God's people.*

(*New Rite of Pastoral Care for the Sick*, 1983)

THE ORDER OF SERVICE

1 Greeting and blessing with holy water
2 Confession
3 Reading from the Gospels
4 Prayers of intercession
5 Laying on of hands, prayer
6 Blessing the oil
7 Anointing the head and hands
8 Prayer for the sick
9 The Lord's Prayer
10 Blessing

Prayer for the sick

*Watch, dear Lord
With those who wake, and watch, and weep
tonight,
And give your angels charge over those who sleep.
Tend your sick ones, O Lord Christ,
Rest your weary ones.
Soothe your suffering ones.
Pity your afflicted ones.
Shield your joyous ones,
And all for your love's sake,
Amen.*

(St Augustine of Hippo in *Together in Prayer*, 1993)

REFLECTION

Do not neglect your sick and elderly. Do not turn away from the handicapped and the dying. Do not push them to the margins of society. For if you do, you will fail to understand that they represent an important truth…that weakness is a creative part of human living.

(Pope John Paul II at
St George's Cathedral, Southwark, 1982)

CLASS DEBATE

Hold a debate on Pope John Paul's words:

This house does not agree that 'Weakness is a creative part of human living'.

Two people should propose the motion and two should oppose it.

THINGS TO DO

▶ Choose a healing story in one of the Gospels. Read the story carefully. Imagine you are that healed person. Write a letter to a friend describing what happened and your feelings.

▶ Write a prayer for the sick that could be used in your school assembly.

The seven sacraments looked at in Units 14–20 are all recognized as such by the Catholic and Orthodox Christians. Other Christians (Protestant, Free Churches) acknowledge only two of them as sacraments – Baptism and Eucharist – because these are the only ones explicitly associated with Jesus in the Gospels. This does not mean that such Christians do not respect ceremonies like confirmation, marriage and ordination as sacred and holy. These Christians also share with Catholics a large number of 'sacramentals' i.e. signs and symbols that point the way to God and express in a concrete and visual way (like an embrace) what words sometimes cannot express.

Baptism ceremonies are called christenings in most other churches. The word means 'putting on Christ'.

There are variations in the way Christians celebrate the Eucharist:

- Orthodox Christians call it 'The Liturgy'
- the Church of England calls it the 'Communion Service'
- Non-conformists describe it as 'The Lord's Supper'.

THINGS TO DO

▶ The illustration below shows 20 Christian symbols. See if you can name them. Then make a list and find out the meaning of each one. Most Christian groups use all of these symbols.

Twenty Christian symbols

TEST YOUR KNOWLEDGE OF THE SACRAMENTS

When you have read Part 3, test your knowledge of the sacraments.

1. Look at the photo above left and answer the following questions:
   a Describe what is happening during Mass.
   b Why do Catholics believe that this is the most sacred part of the Mass? (If you are not sure turn to Unit 22 for more information.)
   c How is the sacrament of the Eucharist related to the Mass?
   d Do you think that women should be more involved in celebrating the Mass?

2. Look at the photo above right and answer the following questions:
   a What part is the priest playing at this wedding?
   b Describe the marriage service as it is celebrated in the Catholic Church.
   c Catholics are not allowed to be remarried in church if they have been divorced. From what you have read in Unit 18, can you suggest reasons for this ruling?
   d How would you reply to someone who says, 'I don't want the fuss of a church wedding'?

3 Roman Catholics celebrate seven sacraments. Two are pictured on this page. Which are the other five?
   a Select one of the five. Find a picture or photograph of the sacrament, or draw a picture.
   b Make this into a work-card to be used by teachers when preparing young children for receiving the sacraments, by writing three or four questions underneath it. Remember the children who use these cards will be about 7 years old.
   c On a separate sheet, write an answer card.
   d Swap cards (to check that your explanations are easily understood).

The Mass is the usual name given to the celebration of the Eucharist in the Catholic Church. In this unit, we look at four aspects of it.

1 THE MASS AS PASSOVER

At Mass, Catholics perform what Jesus did on the night before he died. He celebrated the Passover meal, as all Jews have done (and still do) every springtime. Jews celebrate their escape from slavery in Egypt. They believe that God rescued them, and under the guidance of Moses helped them to 'pass over' into freedom. Each celebration of Passover is seen as making that event real again, bringing the past into the present.

'You must celebrate this day as a religious festival, to remind you of what I, the Lord, have done. Celebrate it for all time to come.'

(*Exodus 12:14*)

Read chapter 12:1–14 in *Exodus*.

'I have so wanted to eat this Passover meal with you.'

(*Luke 22:15*)

2 THE MASS AS SACRIFICE

At this last supper with his friends, Jesus gave the Passover celebration a new meaning. The bitter bread not only represented the slave food which the Jews had eaten in Egypt; it was now broken to represent Jesus' own body which would the next day be broken on the cross. The cup of wine was poured to represent Jesus' own blood which would the next day be poured out in death. This is what Jesus wanted the Passover to mean in the future.

He took a piece of bread, gave thanks to God, broke it, and gave it to them saying, 'This is my body, which is given for you. Do this in memory of me.' In the same way, he gave them the cup after the supper, saying, 'This cup is God's new covenant sealed with my blood, which is poured out for you.'

(*Luke 22:19–20*)

Read *Luke 22:1–20*.

3 THE MASS AS THANKSGIVING

The Greek word *Eucharist* means 'thanksgiving'. The main emotion that the Mass is meant to arouse is not dutiful gloom or sorrow, but joy, wonder, praise and thanks to God for sending Jesus to make us free.

*'Give thanks to the Lord,
because he is good;
his love is eternal.'
Repeat these words in praise to the Lord,
all you whom he has saved.
He has rescued you from your enemies
and has brought you back from foreign countries,
from east and west, from north and south.*

(*Psalm 107(106):1–3*)

4 THE MASS AS FOOD

The Mass comes to a climax at communion, where the bread and wine, which are sacramental signs of Jesus' lifegiving death, are given to the congregation as food and drink. This is so that they too can share in the risen life of Christ.

*'I am the bread of life,
He who comes to me will never be hungry,
He who believes in me will never thirst.'*

(*John 6:35*)

AN OUTLINE OF THE CELEBRATION OF MASS

1 **Opening prayers**
- Confession of sin
- Praise of God
- A prayer to collect these thoughts together

2 **The Word of God**
- Readings
- Gospel
- Sermon
- Creed
- Bidding prayers

3 The Holy Meal

- People's offerings are brought to the altar
- Song of praise
- Eucharistic prayer of thanksgiving*
- The *Our Father*
- Sign of peace
- Communion

4 Closing prayers

- Blessing
- 'Sending out' to serve the Lord

* At the centre of this eucharistic prayer are the words of **consecration**. Catholics believe that when these words are spoken, the substance of the bread and wine becomes the substance of the Body and Blood of Christ, and that he is thus present on the altar.

THINGS TO DO

▶ Outline in your notebooks the four aspects of the Mass. Use your own words.

▶ In groups produce a wall chart to show (with illustrations) the parts of the Mass.

▶ What do you think Hugh Lavery means by: 'The Mass badly represented may be constructed as magic'? Is he right in saying that young people need the transcendent? Where might they find it?

REFLECTIONS

A priest remembers: 'We used to say Mass with our backs to the congregation. Then after Vatican II we turned the altar round and faced the people. I'll never forget how one shocked parishioner came to me. "Father" he said, "I was convinced that when you raised your arms at the consecration of the host, this Bread of Heaven came miraculously down from God into your hands. Now I see you had it there all the time." But I tell you one thing, this good man still comes to Mass. His faith was not shaken!'

The Mass badly represented may be constructed as magic... When do children and teenagers cease going to Mass? Perhaps they cease going to Mass when they no longer believe in magic. But their need for the transcendent, for a more spacious experience of living, still lingers. They still want the transcendent, they still want this contact with a power beyond the finite.

(Hugh Lavery, *Sacraments*, 1982)

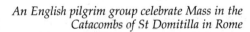

An English pilgrim group celebrate Mass in the Catacombs of St Domitilla in Rome

Prayer is essential for all Christians. They believe it is communication with God. St. Thérèse of Lisieux described it as 'A surge of the heart; it is a simple look turned towards heaven, it is a cry of recognition and of love, embracing both trial and joy.'

Prayer is so important to Christians that they publish more books on this than any other aspect of their faith. The *Catechism of the Catholic Church* devotes a large section to prayer – which leading theologians, like Bernard Häring, say is the best part of the document. This is what it says by way of an introduction:

Prayer is the life of the new heart. It ought to animate us at every moment...

The Tradition of the Church proposes to the faithful certain rhythms of praying intended to nourish continual prayer. Some are daily, such as morning and evening prayer, grace before and after meals, the Liturgy of Hours. Sundays, centred on the Eucharist, are kept holy primarily by prayer. The cycle of the liturgical year and its great feasts are also basic rhythms of the Christian's life of prayer.

The Lord leads all persons by paths and in ways pleasing to him, and each believer responds according to his heart's resolve and the personal expressions of prayer. However, Christian tradition has retained three major expressions of prayer: vocal, meditative and contemplative.

(*Catechism of the Catholic Church*, No.s 2697–9)

Nuns at prayer

A quiet moment of prayer at Mass

VOCAL PRAYER

This is prayer which uses words and the voice. Families may say such prayers together, perhaps before meals. In Catholic schools vocal prayers are usually said at the beginning of the day. Even MPs are led in vocal prayer at the beginning of each day's work at the House of Commons. Many Catholics, especially priests and the religious, say the daily Prayer of the Church known as the Divine Office. It is divided up for different hours of the day. Catholics and other Christians are most familiar with Vespers and Compline, because they are often sung in the great cathedrals on Sundays. Many other popular Catholic vocal prayers are found in this book (e.g. see pages 21 and 52).

MEDITATIONAL PRAYER

Meditation is a prayer of the mind – thinking about God. Christians have always prayed in this way. They think about the words of the Scripture, reflecting especially on the life of Jesus and what it means. Orthodox Christians use icons for this purpose – a practice also increasingly popular among Catholics. Over the centuries, spiritual writers have offered help to ordinary people who think that meditation is difficult. Today one such popular Catholic writer is the cookery expert Delia Smith. Probably most people meditate without even realizing it:

> *'Dear God, I have got to know something. What is it like in heaven? I know its nice but what kind of nice? What happens when it rains?'*

> (Marty, aged 5)

CONTEMPLATIVE PRAYER

An elderly man sitting at the back of the church was asked by his priest what he was doing there. He replied: 'I look at him and he looks at me.' Contemplative prayer, like this, is silent; it is an expression of love. People in love tell you that they do not need to talk, it is enough to be together. Contemplative prayer is:

> *A gaze of faith fixed on Jesus, an attentiveness to the Word of God, a silent love. It achieves real union with a prayer of Christ to the extent that it makes us share in his mystery.*

> (*Catechism of the Catholic Church*, No. 2724)

This kind of prayer is not just for the mystics, like Julian of Norwich (see page 27). Young people are attracted to understand it. They go in thousands to Taizé in France to share silent prayer with the monks (see page 59).

There are also more **vocations** to contemplative religious life than to active religious orders (see page 85).

THINGS TO DO

▶ Find out all you can about the following:

1 Prayer of Petition (Bidding Prayers)
2 The Divine Office (Prayer of the Church)
3 Icons
4 The mystics
5 Gregorian chant.

The local Catholic church may have a library which could help you.

▶ Write about 50 words describing the three types of prayer covered in this unit. Use your own words.

▶ A friend has bought a CD of the now famous Benedictine monks of Santo Domingo de Silos in Spain. The chants are taken from prayers in the Mass. Explain to your friend why the monks spend time praying.

Kieran, a sixth-former from Notre Dame High School, Norwich, made his first trip to Lourdes as a helper (brancardier) on the Diocesan Pilgrimage. Here is an extract from his diary.

Diary of a brancardier (helper) at Lourdes

Thursday, 27 August: *Another scorcher and another hard day – by this time I was seriously lacking sleep. An early start – the sick had to be in the underground basilica for 7.30 am Mass in which they were anointed. Again a full array of bishops present. After a musical reflection and lunch, there was the choice of taking the sick to the Stations of the Cross or a Children's Mass. Myself being a child at heart, chose the Children's Mass. It was brilliant, even though the children ran riot! The Gospel was acted out and the children took an active part. (It was the Gospel of the children going to Jesus, but being turned away by the disciples.) When the children eventually get to Jesus – played by a bearded priest – dozens of them swarmed him and knocked the poor man over – highly amusing. Being our last night in Lourdes, it is apparently customary for the brancs and handmaids to party all night and not to go to bed – the theory being that we could catch up on sleep on the train home. We calmed the party down by visiting the shrine at about 4.30 am and staying until the sun rose – what a night!…*

My verdict: *What a week! Such a brilliant experience. I've made so many friends, including the disabled. Although the work was very, very hard and I was physically exhausted, I feel part of something very special. I've never seen unity like it anywhere before. I recommend the pilgrimage to anyone. Lourdes is a very special place. I can't wait until next year.*

(*Kieran Barnard*)

PILGRIMAGE

People of all ages and all races have always made pilgrimages or journeys to holy places. Kieran went on his pilgrimage to help the sick find peace and companionship. Christian pilgrims have offered numerous reasons for making these prayerful journeys. Here are some of them:

Procession of the sick at Lourdes

- devotion to a particular saint
- curiosity
- to seek healing or ask for favours
- to give thanks for favours received
- as a form of penance for sin
- in the hope of 'earning' eternal life
- to deepen faith
- for companionship.

The Catholic organization CAFOD has recently invited young people to go on Campaign Pilgrimages. Groups walk to shrines in order to experience some hardship and want, in order to 'feel' the suffering of others. This is how one parish took part in CAFOD's campaign for refugees.

Fr Jeff Cridland of St Thomas the Apostle, Peckham, wrote to tell us about his parish's pilgrimage.

'I did not want to go on the Refugee Pilgrimage' he wrote, 'but this was probably a good way to start because a real refugee would have the same feelings multiplied by a hundred. I began to feel better when I saw how many other people had come along. Some were joining a parish venture for the first time.

'Before we started, Susie O'Rawe, our CAFOD Regional Organiser said to me, "You will find it a wonderful experience. I don't know why you will, but you will." She was right. I found that we all entered into an experience that many others have and that we did it with people we could be friends with as we went along.'

(*CAFOD Magazine*, Summer 1994)

Over the years many thousands of Roman Catholic pilgrims have travelled to the Holy Land (where they have joined many other Christians and Jews), to Rome (because of its connection with St Peter and the popes) and to many shrines of Mary across the world.

SHRINES OF MARY

The most popular pilgrim routes take Catholics to:

- Lourdes, France, where St Bernadette is believed to have had visions of Mary who told her to dig for water. The spring is famous for its healing powers.

- Walsingham, the East Anglian shrine, where in AD 1061 it is believed Richeldis of Faversham was told by Mary to build a replica of the Nazareth house where the **Annunciation** to Mary took place.

- Fatima, Portugal, where in 1917 children claim to have had a vision of Mary who asked for prayers and penance.

- Medjugorje, former Yugoslavia. In this war-torn country a group of young people continue to claim that they have had visions of Mary since 1981.

REFLECTION

Pilgrimage

'Where are you going?'
'From nowhere to somewhere.'
'How long will it take you?'
'From now until then.'
'What will you find there?'
'The past as a present.'
'How will you use it?'
'I know not. Amen.'

'What are you packing?'
'A suitcase of sleeping.'
'Why is it heavy?'
'It bulges with night.'
'In what is its value?'
'Goods one can trade with.'
'How will you bargain?'
'I know not. Amen'

'Who will go with you?'
'A child and an old man.'
'How will they travel?'
'On the backs of the dead.'
'What will they live on?'
'Bread, wine and blessings.'
'Will they survive then?'
'I trust so. Amen.'

'What will the land be?'
'Sand, thorns and granite.'
'Why do you want it?'
'As the garden I need.'
'How will you shape it?'
'With songs keen as thistles.'
'When will it flower?'
'From now until then.'

(Nadine Brummer)

FIND OUT

Find out all you can about one place of pilgrimage.

THINGS TO DO

▶ Imagine you are a newspaper reporter visiting a Catholic shrine. Write a report including the following:
  - the history of the shrine
  - at least two interviews with pilgrims
  - several reasons why people have gone there
  - your own comment about their faith.

▶ The Catholic Church refers to itself as 'a pilgrim church'. Why do you think this is? Does Nadine Brummer's poem help you with an answer?

▶ 'You must be either mad or superstitious to go on a pilgrimage.' Write a conversation between two people – one who supports this view and the friend who disagrees.

Of all the saints in the Christian Church, there is none more honoured in both the Orthodox and Roman Catholic traditions than Mary, mother of Jesus. Catholics call her 'Our Lady'. She is given the extraordinary title '**Mother of God**' – extraordinary because God is 'without beginning'. The title, subject of many **icons**, is given to her because Christians believe with St Paul that the fulness of God dwelt in Jesus:

> *For it was by God's own decision that the Son has in himself the full nature of God.*
>
> (Colossians 1:19)

As Jesus' mother, Mary is called *Theotokos*, a Greek word meaning the God-bearer.

One of Mary's major feasts is 'Lady Day' on 25 March. This is also called the Annunciation (the announcement) and on this day the story of the angel announcing to Mary the future birth of Jesus is retold. The Catholic prayer '**Hail Mary**' echoes the angel's greeting.

> *Hail, Mary, full of grace,*
> *the Lord is with thee.*
> *Blessed art thou among women,*
> *and blessed is the fruit of thy womb, Jesus.*
> *Holy Mary, Mother of God,*
> *pray for us sinners, now,*
> *and at the hour of our death.*
> *Amen.*

Three aspects of Mary are celebrated in the titles that have been given to her by the Church, which sees Mary as having achieved what all Christians hope one day to be:

1 Her **Immaculate Conception** speaks of the purity or sinlessness without which no one can enter into the presence of God.
2 Her **virginity** speaks of a Christ who is born into the world, not as the result of human merit or effort, but as a totally gracious gift from God.
3 Her **Assumption** into heaven speaks of the overcoming of death, and the union of body and soul with God, for which all Christians yearn.

THE ROSARY

In the Catholic Church there has recently been a revival of interest in the custom of reciting the 'Hail Mary' 50 times, while beads are counted off on a string. This is called the **Rosary**. The tradition began in the thirteenth century when devotion to Mary came under attack. Gospel stories of the life of Jesus – joyful, sorrowful and glorious (see below) – are meditated upon, while the words of the prayer are repeated over and over again. Once very popular, the rosary went out of fashion after the Second Vatican Council. But Pope John Paul II has revived it. In 1994 the Spanish CD label Divusca recorded the Pope's rosary and made it into a hit!

THE JOYFUL MYSTERIES

- The Annunciation – *Luke 1:26–38*
- The Visitation – *Luke 1:39–47*
- The Nativity – *Luke 2:1–7*
- The Presentation – *Luke 2:22–32*
- The Finding in the Temple – *Luke 2:41–9*

THE SORROWFUL MYSTERIES

- The Agony in the garden – *Luke 22:39–44*
- The Scourging at the pillar – *Luke 23:20–3*
- The Crowning with thorns – *Mark 15:15–20*
- The Carrying of the cross – *Luke 23:26–34*
- Jesus dies on the cross – *Luke 23:34–46*

THE GLORIOUS MYSTERIES

- Jesus is raised from the dead – *Mark 16:1–6*
- The Ascension – *Acts 1:9–12*
- The Coming of the Spirit – *Acts 2:1–22*
- The Assumption of Mary – *Psalm 45:10–17*
- The Coronation of Mary – *Revelation 12:1–5*

A prayer often used by Catholics

Hail, holy Queen, Mother of Mercy! Hail, our life, our sweetness and our hope. To thee do we cry, poor banished children of Eve; to thee do we send up our sighs, mourning and weeping in this vale of tears.

Turn then, most gracious advocate, thine eyes of mercy towards us; and after this our exile, show unto us the blessed fruit of thy womb, Jesus. O clement, O loving, O sweet Virgin Mary.

Pray for us, O holy Mother of God

That we may be made worthy of the promises of Christ.

A 15th century painting of the Annunciation

REFLECTION

The Baker-Woman

The baker-woman in her humble lodge
Received the grain of wheat from God,
For nine whole months the grain she stored:
Behold the handmaid of the Lord.
Make us the bread, Mary, Mary,
Make us the bread, we need to be fed.

The baker-woman took the road which led
To Bethlehem, the House of Bread.
To knead the bread she laboured through
*   the night*
And brought it forth about midnight.
Bake us the bread, Mary, Mary,
Bake us the bread, we need to be fed.

(Marie Noel, translated by H J Richards)

THINGS TO DO

▶ What feast of Our Lady is represented in the painting? Describe the story in your own words.

▶ You are a Catholic. Your friend who is not, asks you to tell her what a rosary is. What would you say?

▶ 'Catholics venerate (are devoted to) Mary; they do not worship her.' What do Catholics mean when they say this?

▶ The Pope says that 'Our Lady' should be a model for every Catholic woman. What do you think he means?

The Church, in the course of the year, unfolds the whole mystery of Christ from his Incarnation and Nativity through his Ascension, to Pentecost and the expectation of the blessed hope of the coming of the Lord.

(*Catechism of the Catholic Church*, No. 1194)

THE CHRISTIAN YEAR

As the chart shows, the Christian liturgical year is divided into seasons, each commemorating an important event in the life of Christ. Easter is the major Christian Feast but the Church year begins with the winter celebration of **Advent** and **Christmas**.

Advent and Christmas

Christmas was introduced late into the calendar, taking over from the Roman holiday of midwinter's day on 25 December. It has a four-week preparation period called Advent, which means 'coming'. The Scripture readings speak not only of Jesus' birth but refer to his longed-for coming at the end of time. Catholic customs include the Advent wreath with candles which represent Christ as the Light of the World; Advent calendars with 24 picture windows to be opened day by day; carols retelling the Gospel stories of Christ's birth; and the building of Christmas cribs, a devotion first introduced by St Francis of Assisi.

The first Christmas mass is celebrated as the day begins, at midnight, with the joyful greeting of 'Immanuel' – God is with us.

Lent and Easter

Easter day also is celebrated in a night vigil. This service is the most important celebration in the Church's year. It begins with a fire lit outside the church, and the procession of the Easter Candle entering the darkened building to show that, in the resurrection of Jesus, light has overcome darkness. It is an appropriate occasion for new baptisms. It is a time of joyful celebration when the choir and people sing 'Christ is risen, he is risen indeed'. Children have Easter eggs as symbols of tombs from which new life springs.

Like Christmas, the feast of Easter has a long preparation period – 40 days known as **Lent** (from Old English for springtime when days began to

A simplified plan of the liturgical year

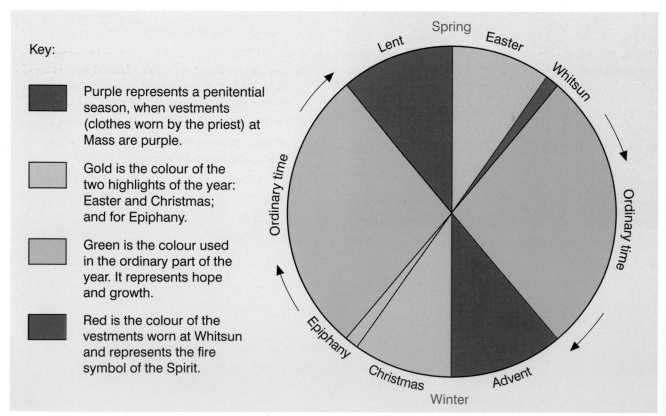

Key:

Purple represents a penitential season, when vestments (clothes worn by the priest) at Mass are purple.

Gold is the colour of the two highlights of the year: Easter and Christmas; and for Epiphany.

Green is the colour used in the ordinary part of the year. It represents hope and growth.

Red is the colour of the vestments worn at Whitsun and represents the fire symbol of the Spirit.

The congregation renew their baptism vows at the Easter Mass

lengthen). It is a time of prayer, fasting and serious self-discipline. Lent begins on **Ash Wednesday** and comes to a climax with Holy Week:

- **Palm Sunday** recalls the arrival of Jesus in Jerusalem.
- **Maundy Thursday** commemorates the Last Supper of Jesus and his washing of the disciples' feet.

- **Good Friday** relives the day when Jesus gave his life for his beliefs. Christians claim that this death is the salvation of the world.
- **Holy Saturday** is a day of quiet waiting for the good news of resurrection.

Many of the other feasts shown on the chart are described elsewhere in the book.

A hot summer's day. Children in their First Communion clothes. Bright flowers everywhere. Clergy in their most decorative vestments. A solemn procession round the church or convent garden, with gentle songs about the sweet sacrament, and much incense. That is what **Corpus Christi** has meant to generations of Catholics all over the world.

'Corpus Christi' means *Body of Christ*. (Following the Vatican Council the feast was renamed 'Corpus et Sanguis Christi' – the Body and Blood of Christ.) The name refers to the sacrament of the Eucharist in which Catholics believe Christ is present in the form of bread and wine. During the Middle Ages, this sacrament, instituted by Jesus at his last supper (see p. 30) was felt to need its own celebration. A ceremony called **Benediction** (blessing) was devised in which the Mass is, as it were, extended, by displaying the Sacrament in a gold case (called a monstrance) on the altar, as a focus for silent contemplation, prayers of praise and a final blessing.

On the feast of Corpus Christi this blessing is given several times during a solemn procession. In some places (e.g. Arundel in Sussex) the floor is patterned with a carpet of flowers for the procession. The gathering together of the whole community around the sacrament, which is fed to them at Mass, expresses the fact that the people themselves become the Body of Christ. In the words of St Paul:

> *Christ is like a single body, which has many parts; it is still one body, even though it is made up of different parts. In the same way, all of us, whether Jews or Gentiles, whether slaves or free, have been baptized into the one body by the Spirit, and we have all been given the one Spirit to drink…All of you are Christ's body, and each one is part of it.*
>
> (*1 Corinthians 12:12–13*)

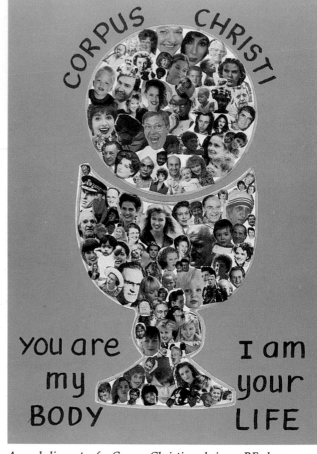

A symbolic poster for Corpus Christi made in an RE class

The poster on this page was produced by some Catholic students in preparation for Corpus Christi. The Reflection on page 57 and the piece of church music (composed for this book) illustrate perfectly the meaning of this feast for Catholics.

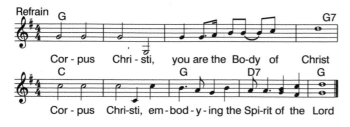

Refrain

Cor - pus Chri - sti, you are the Bo-dy of Christ

Cor - pus Chri-sti, em-bod-y - ing the Spi-rit of the Lord

Verse

Verses

1 Many as you are, you form one *body* in Christ,
   All of you depending *on* each other. (*Romans 12:15*)

2 The loaf of *bread* that you break, Is it not a sharing in the Bo*dy* of Christ? (*1 Corinthians 10:16*)

(Music by H J Richards)

REFLECTION

'I tried to catch your attention this morning. Remember when you came back to your seat and closed your eyes and put your head reverently down and talked and talked to me. I wanted you to listen. I wanted to tell you to open your eyes and look at my broken body all around you…I was the old man in front of you, the unmarried mother at the end of your seat, the family of seven children across the aisle from you – and I almost had the impression you disapproved of me. I was the woman in the green coat whose husband left her this week and whose heart was being eaten out right through Mass and a friendly smile or word would have been a little support to me. I am your wife who cooked and prepared and coped with the children while you read the Sunday newspaper.

I am your husband and your children and you gave us your cold silent treatment and deadened the whole atmosphere of home. I am your mother and father you have ignored and criticized. I am your neighbour whom you spend so much time gossiping about. Please don't keep me at bay any longer. Don't talk to me. Listen. I don't want you to go on loving my spirit and ignoring my body. When will you understand that you cannot have Holy Communion with me if you don't have communion with your brothers and sisters. Stop thinking of me as some kind of spiritual being in the skies. I am one with these people and you cannot have me without them.'

(From *How to Prepare Your Children for Mass*, Veritas Family Resources)

'Don't put your head down and talk to me. Look up and listen.'

THINGS TO DO

▶ Using a concordance, find out all the references to the Body of Christ in Paul's letters. (A concordance is a list of words from the Bible in alphabetical order, with cross references to all the places in the Bible where the words are found.)

▶ How do they reveal what Paul thought about the Church?

▶ Find some people who attended a Catholic parish or school in the 1940s or 1950s. Interview them for their memories about Corpus Christi processions in those days.

The musical tradition of the universal Church is a treasure of immeasurable value, greater even than that of any art. The main reason for this pre-eminence is that, as sacred melody united to words, it forms a necessary or integral part of the solemn liturgy.

(Second Vatican Council, *Liturgy 112*)

Praise of God has always been accompanied by music. Since Old Testament times, communities have sung and played instruments to accompany their prayer. Here are some comments about the styles and effects of church music:

Praise God in his Temple!…
Praise him with trumpets.
Praise him with harps and lyres,
Praise him with drums and dancing.
Praise him with harps and flutes.
Praise him with cymbals,
Praise him with loud cymbals.
Praise the Lord, all living creatures!
Praise the Lord.

(Psalm 150)

'How I wept, deeply moved by your hymns, songs and voices that echoed through your church! What emotion I experienced in them! Those sounds flowed into my ears, distilling the truth in my heart. A feeling of devotion surged within me, and tears streamed down my face – tears that did me good.'

(St Augustine, *Confessions*)

A folk group lead the liturgy at Lourdes

The Church acknowledges Gregorian Chant as proper to the Roman liturgy: therefore, other things being equal, it should be given pride of place in liturgical services.

(Second Vatican Council, *Liturgy 116*)

Gregorian chant is attributed to Pope Gregory the Great who died in AD 604. Many chants used today, however, come from the seventh to ninth centuries. Gregory was important for establishing choirs and choral scholars in the churches of Rome. In the nineteenth century, this chant music was revived by the monks of Solesmes. Today, it has been revived again, for example by the monks of Silos, and even made popular outside the Roman Catholic Church.

In certain parts of the world, especially mission lands, there are peoples who have their own musical traditions, and these play a great part in their religious and social life. For this reason due importance is to be attached to their music… Missionaries…should be competent in promoting the traditional music of these peoples, both in schools and in sacred services.

(Second Vatican Council, *Liturgy 119*)

The Council changed the practice of earlier centuries when Western music was imposed on non-Western peoples. The film *The Mission* illustrated how sixteenth-century missionaries taught Gregorian chant to the native Indian people. This is a far cry from the dancing African nuns who processed to the altar in a recent Mass in Rome, accompanied by African drums.

'I do wish we could sing the old familiar hymns during Mass – with the organ playing. I don't like these new folk groups with their pop-type songs.'

(Elderly parishioner in London parish)

'I like going to Mass now because I play my flute with the folk group. I feel part of what is going on and the singing is more cheerful.'

(13-year-old in a London parish)

Quiet meditation at Taizé

Perhaps the most popular music in the Catholic Church today is the meditative music from Taizé in France. From this mixed community of many different Christian traditions there has come a quiet, simple style of repetitive music that is attractive to all Christian denominations, all ages and all races.

Meditative singing begins with gathering in silence or the repetition of a chant as people arrive. Repetitive chants have a certain element of spontaneity which hymns lack: they last as long as people want to sing.

(Taizé, *Praying Together in Word and Song*, 1989)

Adoramus te Domine

O_____   A-do-ra-mus te Do-mi - ne

We adore you, Lord.

(Taizé)

CLASS DEBATE

Hold a class debate on:

> This house believes that sacred music should have a dignity that folk groups cannot provide.

Two people should propose the motion and two people should oppose it.

THINGS TO DO

▶ Find out more about Taizé. Learn the *Adoramus te Domine* for an assembly.

▶ See how many different styles of church music you can find on tape or CD. Your music and RE teachers may help you. Bring the tapes to class and compare them. Make a chart to show your preferences. Which one did you like least? Say why.

It is hard to believe that until as little as 30 years ago Catholics were forbidden to pray with Christians belonging to other Churches. Special permission had to be sought for a Catholic to attend marriage in another Church. Today all this has changed.

It is a frequent sight on Good Friday to see Christians gather together in town centres to witness their common faith. The two bishops of Liverpool, Catholic and Anglican, have been great examples of shared concern for people in need, a concern which is naturally expressed in shared prayer. Christians today are more faithful than they were in the past to the Gospel Jesus taught everyone to pray:

> *Our Father, who art in heaven,*
> *hallowed be thy name;*
> *thy kingdom come;*
> *thy will be done on earth as it is in heaven.*
> *Give us this day our daily bread;*
> *and forgive us our trespasses,*
> *as we forgive those who trespass against us;*
> *and lead us not into temptation,*
> *but deliver us from evil. Amen.*

There are three important communities of prayer that welcome Christians of all denominations. Catholics feel very comfortable in these communities.

- *Taizé*, in France, where Protestant Robert Schutz founded a contemplative community in 1949. Thousands of young people go there every year to pray with the Protestant, Catholic and Orthodox monks.

- *Iona*, an island off the west coast of Scotland on which St Columba built a monastery as early as the sixth century. It is here that John Smith, the former leader of the Labour Party, was buried in 1994.

- *Corrymeela*, in Northern Ireland, where Catholic and Protestant believers meet and pray together for peace.

THINGS TO DO

▶ Research the three places mentioned in this unit. Prepare a short talk for the class.

▶ Write out the 'Our Father' prayer in your own words.

The two bishops of Liverpool with Archbishop Desmond Tutu

TEST YOUR KNOWLEDGE

When you have read Part 4, test your knowledge
on the Church at prayer.

Celebrating the Mass at Lourdes

Celebrating the start of Holy Week in Brazil

A Look at the photo above.

1 Why do people go to Lourdes?
2 What is the purpose of a pilgrimage?
3 Name three other places of pilgrimage
   associated with Our Lady?
4 Why would the Mass always be an important
   part of a pilgrimage?
5 In what way is the Mass a new Passover
   celebration?
6 Why would some Christian pilgrims go to
   Bethlehem in December?
7 Where might Christian pilgrims go in the
   spring holiday?
8 Why do Christians use carols and hymns in
   their worship?
9 What is Gregorian chant?
10 What is meant by 'contemplative' prayer?

B Look at the photo above.

1 What is this celebration called?
2 What event in the life of Jesus is particularly
   remembered on this day?
3 Why is Easter regarded as the most important
   Christian feast?
4 In what way does the Church prepare for this
   feast?
5 Should Easter be a public holiday in Britain?
   Give reasons for your answer.

C Do you think:

● that the traditional self-discipline of Advent
   and Lent (prayer, fasting and giving to
   charity) are helpful to Christians today?

● that Catholics should be encouraged to
   attend Mass every Sunday?

● that everyone should go on at least one
   pilgrimage during their lifetime, believers and
   nonbelievers alike?

● that prayer is an essential part of the life of a
   Christian?

The glory of God is a person fully alive.

(St Irenaeus, second century)

These words, written so early in the life of the Church, could be taken as a motto or emblem for all those thousands of Christians who work for the good of other people. At the heart of all Catholic social teaching is the conviction that each person is unique; that each person is created in the image of God; and that all people could reflect the glory of God himself, if they could live a life whole and undistorted by sin, poverty and lack of freedom.

One of the most memorable passages in English was written by John Donne, Dean of St Paul's Cathedral in London in the seventeenth century. A great bell was tolling for a funeral. As he heard it he was going to ask who was being buried that day, when the thought struck him:

No man is an island, entire of itself. Any man's death diminishes me because I am involved in mankind. And therefore never send to know for whom the bell tolls. It tolls for thee.

Catholic social teaching is based on these two ideas: each individual is an image of God and each human being is responsible for all the rest.

KEY WORD

Social ethics – the ethics or moral behaviour, not simply of individuals, but of society itself. The conduct of groups of people at the local, national and international level. Social ethics is about behaviour between people, and how they should behave towards the natural world and towards animals.

Each individual is an image of God and each human being is responsible for all the rest

REFLECTIONS

The dignity of the human person requires the pursuit of the common good. Everyone should be concerned to create and support institutions that improve the conditions of human life.

Respect for the human person proceeds by way of respect for the principle that 'everyone should look upon his neighbour' (without any exception) as 'another self', above all bearing in mind his life and the means necessary for living it with dignity. No legislation could by itself do away with the fears, prejudices, and attitudes of pride and selfishness which obstruct the establishment of truly fraternal societies. Such behaviour will cease only through the charity that finds in every one a 'neighbour', a brother or sister.

(*Catechism of the Catholic Church*, No.s 1926, 1931)

Catholics are not the only people deeply concerned about human dignity. The views outlined by the Catechism are echoed in the documents of many other Christian Churches. Humanists and others, of all faiths or none, work for the good of the human race too. But in Part 5 we will look at the work of Roman Catholics based on the compassion which the Gospel commands them to practise. Later in the book we will analyse the moral law itself (see Unit 48).

◇

TALKING POINTS

'Look at you comfortable Christians carrying the cross. You don't know anything about suffering, in your cosy homes and your cars and your jobs. I don't believe in your God – you say he is a God of Love. Rubbish, I know.'

(A homeless man watching the procession of the cross in Norwich on Good Friday.)

'I feel that what we are doing is just a drop in the ocean. But if that drop was not in the ocean, I think the ocean would be less because of that missing drop. I do not agree with the big way of doing things. To us what matters is an individual.'

(Mother Teresa)

Christ has no body on earth but yours, no hands but yours, no feet but yours.
Yours are the eyes through which must look out Christ's compassion on the world.
Yours are the feet with which he is to go about doing good.
Yours are the hands with which he blesses now.

(Teresa of Avila)

THINGS TO DO

▶ Explain in your words what is meant by the Church's social teaching.

▶ Design a poster including Teresa of Avila's words.

▶ What do Catholics mean by the 'Dignity of the Human Person'?

The duty of making oneself a neighbour to others and actively serving them becomes even more urgent when it involves the disadvantaged, in whatever area this may be. 'As you did it to one of the least of these my brethren, you did it to me.'

(Catechism of the Catholic Church, No. 1932)

CAFOD stands for the *Catholic Fund for Overseas Development*. It is the official agency of the Catholic Church in England and Wales, set up in 1962 by the Catholic bishops. It helps to raise funds to support projects for the disadvantaged overseas. The organization describes itself this way:

CAFOD aims to help people help themselves, involving the local community to the greatest extent possible. Projects are concerned with the causes, as well as the conditions of hunger, disease, ignorance and poverty. CAFOD's goal is: to promote human development and social justice in witness to Christian faith and gospel values. CAFOD supports over 1000 projects in 75 countries.

The Irish Church's agency is called *Trocaire* (which is the Irish word for 'mercy'). It very often works alongside CAFOD.

FUND RAISING

Every year Catholics in every parish and in many schools take part in a national fund-raising campaign. It is quite simple – a family fast day. Envelopes are distributed in churches and schools and people are encouraged to go without food and contribute the cost to the fund. In this way, almost all the money raised, about £20 million per year, is used for the projects themselves and not in administration.

CAFOD also takes part in the major national appeals following worldwide tragedies. Many Catholics send donations for help following earthquakes, war disasters – such as in Rwanda in Africa – or famine through CAFOD.

THE PROJECTS

CAFOD sends aid to about 75 countries in the developing world. Many different projects benefit from CAFOD's work:

- clean water
- food production
- health care
- adult education
- technical skills
- community development.

The purpose of these projects is to give aid that lasts. 'If you give a man a fish, he will eat once. If you teach a man to fish, he will eat for the rest of his life.'

The Misereor hunger cloth from Haiti

EDUCATING PEOPLE IN BRITAIN

One of the main tasks of CAFOD is to educate the first world about the third world. Over the years, CAFOD has produced valuable and colourful materials on many issues. Its books, pamphlets, posters and videos are widely used in schools. Each year a theme is selected and material offered for study groups or classes so that every aspect of a problem is considered. CAFOD is not afraid to point out the weaknesses of past secular and religious ignorance. During the 1992 Columbus celebrations, for example, CAFOD's material revealed the terrible abuse of the Indian people by the Catholic Church.

The picture opposite shows one of the 'hunger cloths' or 'prayer cloths' distributed by CAFOD on behalf of Germany's sister organization, *Misereor*. These large cloth hangings are produced by Catholic artists to represent a biblical reflection on world issues. This one is called 'Tree of Life' and was designed by the Haitian artist, Jacques Chery. It expresses the suffering of people like his own and he places that suffering at the foot of the cross.

FOR DISCUSSION

Here are some questions asked by people today. Divide into groups of four and discuss them.

▶ Why don't some of the countries help themselves instead of asking for overseas aid?

▶ Why doesn't our government give more overseas aid? It seems to be charities that do all the work.

▶ How can we be sure that our money reaches the people who need it?

▶ Why do we give money to help victims of war when the people refuse to stop fighting?

▶ Why do so many children end up on the streets?

▶ Does the media report tragedies accurately or is the coverage just trying to be sensational?

FOR DISCUSSION

The following is part of a newspaper article that appeared at the height of the rescue appeals for war and disease victims in Rwanda.

COMPANY POCKETS 50p FROM EVERY RWANDA DONATION

Interactive Telephone Service (ITS) receives 50p for each call giving a credit-card donation it takes on Rwanda Crisis hotlines, the Red Cross said. It has handled tens of thousands of calls prompted by newspaper advertisements and television appeals from members of the Disasters Emergency Committee, an umbrella organization for seven charities including the Red Cross, Christian Aid and Action Aid.

(*Independent on Sunday*, August 1994)

Two replies to this are possible:

● 'Scandal! The same company lost money on a phone-in game accused of being an illegal lottery, and now appears to be using people's tragedy to make money.'

● 'What's wrong? The appeal is within the Charity Commission's guidelines. ITS can guarantee a prompt service and only 50p per caller is lost to the cause.'

▶ Discuss the issue in your groups.

THINGS TO DO

Send a stamped, self-addressed envelope to CAFOD, Romero Close, Stockwell Road, London SW9 9TY for information about its work with schools or for its free schools' pack. (One representative of your class should write for all of you.)

▶ Distribute the information received and produce a display board.

The child is entitled to receive education, which shall be free and compulsory, at least in the elementary stages.

(*United Nations Declaration*)

It is more than 35 years since the UN made this statement in its Declaration of the Rights of the Child, but there are still 715 million children in the world who have no schools to attend.

Christian Churches have consistently appealed and worked for human rights for children, not least in the matter of education.

Each individual is truly a person, with a nature that is endowed with intelligence and free will, and rights and duties… These rights and duties are universal and inviolable.

(Pope John XXIII)

The Catholic Church has been inseparably involved in the development of education in Europe in the past and in the developing world today. This is mainly due to the sense of vocation which has inspired individuals to serve God as teachers.

In the Catholic Church there are many religious orders whose particular gift (charism) lies in education. These orders all owe their inspiration to St Benedict who wrote his famous rule for monks at Monte Cassino, Italy, 1400 years ago. St Benedict's monks were the first educators of Europe, teaching people to read and write and to keep reliable records for libraries. From Bede of Jarrow (d. AD 735) to Cardinal Basil Hume of Westminster (a monk of Ampleforth Abbey), the Benedictines have been outstanding ambassadors of good education.

A different wave of Christian education swept across Europe in the eighteenth and nineteenth centuries, led by priests, brothers and nuns responding to the changes brought about by urban development. Large populations brought great poverty, and many Catholics felt called to respond by setting up 'poor schools' for victims of the new industrial regimes.

THREE EXAMPLES OF CATHOLIC EDUCATION

1   At Bosa, Bogotà in Colombia

During the nineteenth-century Industrial Revolution, a German Catholic family called Fey broke from the growing trend to put profit before people and refused to employ children in its factory. A daughter of the family, Clare, was inspired to go

Sister Claudia Angelica, a Sister of the Poor Child Jesus, with Colombian children

one step further – she founded a poor school in the town of Aachen. It was the beginning of the Religious Congregation of the Sisters of the Poor Child Jesus. This was 150 years ago. Over the years, thousands of children have been educated by the sisters in many countries, including Britain. Today, as with many other religious orders, the schools in Britain are run by lay staff and are in the hands of the diocese.

But in South America Clare Fey's sisters still run schools, mainly in the shanty towns or in the poorest parts of large cities. With help from the Congregation in Europe, the Colombian-born sisters are able to educate the poor.

2   At Ampleforth College

Ampleforth College, an independent Roman Catholic boarding school for boys, overlooks a beautiful valley in North Yorkshire. It is a unique

Boys at Ampleforth College

example of Benedictine education – probably the best of its kind. The school has a staff ratio of 1:9 and caters for more than 650 boys. The upper school is divided into ten houses, a most important feature in the school because it nurtures community identity. This is a feature in all boarding schools, but Ampleforth is unique because of the relationship between the individual houses and the central monastic community, of which eight out of ten housemasters are members. The houses are mostly physically distinct with their own chapels, common rooms, dormitories and study areas. The ideals of the school are rich in Benedictine tradition:

> *The aim of the school is to share with parents, staff and above all boys, the values upon which the monastic community is founded: the desire for truth, unaffected faith in God, respect for others, especially the vulnerable and the ordinary, the sense of belonging, care for material things, space to grow, the search for the difficult balance between order and liberty.*
>
> (Ampleforth College brochure)

Boys attending Ampleforth are highly privileged. They are given the best educational opportunities. For many Catholic families the greatest privilege is the participation of the boys in the Benedictine monastic spirit.

REFLECTION

'We should always teach children who they are. We should say to each of them, do you know who you are? God created you. You are a marvel, you are unique. In all the world there is no other child like you. In the years that have passed, or in those to come there has never been and will never be another like you. You have the capacity for anything and when you grow up, can you harm another who is like you, a marvel? You must cherish one another, you must work – we must all work – to make this world worthy of its children.'

(Pablo Cassals, quoted in an address given by Albert Price, director of the Catholic Education Service)

3 At Catholic schools in the UK

There are hundreds of Catholic schools in the UK, which work within the state system, offering an education similar to that given in all other state schools. The children, like the junior pupils in the photo, follow all the state education directives. But, in addition, Catholic schools have a distinctive mark – they put spiritual and religious values high in their priorities and the sense of Christian community is the hallmark of their work.

Children at a Roman Catholic school

THINGS TO DO

Look at the photographs on these two pages.

▶ Do you think that all the young people shown need the same basic education?

▶ How is their Catholic school different from other state schools, if at all?

▶ What part did St Benedict play in Catholic education?

'I was hungry and you fed me,
thirsty and you gave me a drink;
I was a stranger and you received me in your
*   homes,*
naked and you clothed me;
I was sick and you took care of me,
in prison and you visited me.'
The righteous will answer him,
'When, Lord, did we ever see you hungry and feed
*   you,*
or thirsty and give you a drink?
When did we ever see you a stranger and welcome
*   you in our homes,*
or naked and clothe you?
When did we ever see you sick or in prison, and
*   visit you?'*
The King will reply, 'I tell you, whenever you did
*   this for one of the least important of these*
*   brothers and sisters of mine, you did it for me!'*

(Matthew 25:31–46)

The problem of homelessness is worse than ever today

For Christians, this is a memorable passage in Matthew's Gospel. It comes at the end of the evangelist's last of five great discourses. It therefore sums up Matthew's vision of Jesus. It is Jesus who will pass God's own judgement on people. He will judge them on only one issue – their loving compassion for others. This, Matthew believes, is the final meaning of the Jewish Law by which Jesus himself had tried to live.

The text leads immediately into the account of Jesus' passion and death. 'The Son of Man' is handed over to be crucified. In other words, Jesus immediately identifies himself with the poor and the outcast, even to the point of being buried in a borrowed grave. Throughout the history of the Church, individuals and groups – usually religious congregations – have thought very seriously about these words. They also form the basis of many official Church pronouncements.

All Christians are called to act.
For stating principles is not enough.
To point out injustice is not enough.
Prophetic cries are not enough.
Words lack weight unless we all become
responsible and act effectively.

(Octogesima Adveniens, Pope Paul VI)

This Catholic concern is, of course, echoed by other Christians. The charity Christian Aid spearheads the work for the Protestant Churches, and Tear Fund is the official agency for Evangelical Christians, such as the pop star Cliff Richard. These agencies often work side by side with the Catholic CAFOD and Trocaire (Irish) charities.

In recent times, the Churches have frequently worked side by side on social issues. The history of the national charity, Shelter, is an example of this. It was formed in 1966 when five charities came together to start a campaign for housing the homeless. They were: the Housing Societies Fund Charitable Trust, Christian Action, Housing the Homeless Central Fund, British Churches Housing Trust and the Catholic Housing Aid Society.

◇

THE HOMELESS

Shelter was started quite deliberately at Christmas, a time when people generally feel generous and are aware of the homeless and refugees, which is the very theme of the Christmas story. People responded immediately and £200,000 was raised in the first year. It was given to non-profit-making housing associations, which bought houses, repaired them and then let them out at reasonable rents. There were high hopes that homelessness could shortly become a thing of the past. But 30 years later, the problem is worse than ever. Shelter still exists and often enters into political argument with the government over the low priority given to housing. Church leaders sometimes join in this debate with politicians (see Unit 56).

A former Director of Shelter, Neil McIntosh, praised young people for their support of the campaign:

> *Over the years Shelter has been a young people's campaign. The involvement of unpaid helpers of all ages, particularly young people, has been essential. These people have performed wonders. They have raised huge sums of money, put constant pressure on local councils and provided housing aid services in their spare time. In many cases they have taken people in urgent need into their own homes.*

THE HOMELESS WORLDWIDE

One of CAFOD's recent campaigns has focused on the homeless and the refugees. It sees problems on three fronts:

1   The breakdown of whole societies because of power struggles or outright war. Pictures of exhausted refugees on the move are all too familiar on the television screen.
2   The breakdown of family life, which brings about an increasing number of young homeless people in our major cities.
3   The new Criminal Justice and Public Order Bill, recently introduced by the UK government, which is likely to aggravate the problems of travellers in the UK. CAFOD has highlighted the particular problems for the 10,000 Irish travellers, mainly Roman Catholics, who find it difficult to find places on local authority caravan sites. Many other groups, such as the New-Age travellers, will suffer under the new legislation.

THINGS TO DO

▶ Why do people become homeless? List as many reasons as you can, then compare your list with three others. In this group, design a poster showing the problem.

▶ Plan a short project on one aspect of homelessness. Research the topic by contacting Shelter, or CAFOD, or your local authority, or by using material in the school and public libraries.

▶ Hold a class discussion on the problems of homelessness and young people. Why do they leave home? What happens then?

'I was homeless and you sheltered me'

When the heads of governments met in Rio de Janeiro, in 1993, many young people wrote to Prime Minister John Major and to the Brazilian Ambassador, calling for some action to be taken on behalf of street children. It had become known that Rio officials (government and police) were shooting homeless children, to clean up the streets for the visit. This 'cleansing' still goes on.

Alongside this tragedy, and perhaps because of it, there is a growing concern for the world's poorest children. Millions of them live without adult care, in gutters, in sewers, in doorways – chased by business-people and police, and forced into glue-sniffing, drug-taking, theft and prostitution.

Here are some of the responses that Catholics have recently made to this enormous problem.

MARK IN INDIA

Mark Spring was studying for his A levels, when Brother Gregory visited his school to talk about the Lasallian Developing World Projects. This scheme, organized by the Catholic De La Salle Brothers, sends young volunteers during their summer holidays to work on

Mark with the children he helped in Suranam, India

building sites in Africa, Asia or the Caribbean. Instructed by local craftsmen, and accompanied by teachers, they build classrooms, offices and houses for the local community. Mark gained a place on one of these schemes and went to Suranam, India, for six weeks to build a schoolroom. It was so rewarding that he then put his university place on hold and returned for a year to teach football to former street children. He has just returned with his vision enlarged and his values on human life readjusted. Mark says: 'I have had to revise all my ideas about what is really important in life. I sometimes feel ashamed now of the way I took so much for granted.'

FATHER PETER WALTERS IN COLOMBIA, SOUTH AMERICA

Fr Peter was an Anglican priest serving pilgrims at the shrine in Walsingham. But he returned, whenever he could, to the streets of Medellin, in Colombia. There as a student traveller he had been

Father Peter Walters with street children in Colombia

'adopted' by the street children when he found himself out of funds! He was moved by their plight and felt called to speak out for their rights and their human needs. He set up the charity *Let the Children Live* to help the 'disposable ones', as Colombia's street children are called. He wants to get them off the streets too, but by giving them a home and a future.

Fr Peter has so identified with the children that he recently became a Catholic priest so that he could remain in Colombia (a Catholic country) and work with the Church to care for the outcast children.

ALEX FRYE IN BOLIVIA

A road accident left Alex, aged 18, in intensive care, a friend dead and others injured. The terrible experience made her reassess her life. 'Until that moment', she said, 'everything was for me, get good grades at school, find a job, earn lots of money.'

Then Alex picked up a leaflet at church about a mission in Bolivia twinned with her parish, and served by a Norfolk priest, Fr Pat Cleary. She knew at once that she wanted to volunteer to go out and help the street children of Cochabamba. She joined Sister Stephanie at a

Alex with Bolivian orphans

children's centre, part of the *Amanacer* Project (the word means 'day break') set up in 1981 to help the children. The Project, funded by Catholic parishes and schools, now has an orphanage, workshops, schools and clinics.

Alex spent six months working in the orphanage. 'It was terribly hard work,' she said, 'but wonderful to be with children so badly abused and in need of love.' Her letters describe how they take food out to those remaining on the streets and to those in prison, 'where they wouldn't otherwise eat!'

JAIME JARAMILLO OF BOGOTA, COLOMBIA

It would be wrong to think that only the Western world is concerned about the street children. Colombia has its own hero. Twenty years ago Jaime Jaramillo, a young, fairly wealthy student was shocked at the death of a child knocked down on the roads as she ran to pick up rubbish thrown from a car. She was a 'gamine', a street child. This changed his life. He began to give gifts to hundreds of children, feeding them and putting his own life at risk by speaking out on their behalf. When he discovered, years later, as he paid a hospital bill for Rebecca, aged 11, that she lived underground in the sewers, he swung into action and set up a foundation, *Fundacion Niños de los Andes,* to raise money to rescue the sewer children.

Today, Jaime still spends time in the sewers rescuing children and babies from the filth and danger, and has built a home for hundreds of children. During the day he works as a geophysicist, and his wife and young children agree that 60 per cent of his earnings go to the *Fundacion* children. 'God gave me all the tools to do what he wanted. If I were a poor guy, I would never have been able to do what I have done. If I didn't have money, how could I set up all these things.'

The result of his work speaks for itself. More than 100 former gamines are employed in the oil industry where Jaime is respected; one rescued boy has won a tennis scholarship to Florida; one former drug addict is in the National Youth Orchestra.

Jaime Jaramillo who cares for the sewer children in Bogotà

REFLECTION

My greatest achievement is to have created a social conscience regarding the gamines – not just in Colombia but in other places as well. But what's more important, what I also hope to achieve through our successes, is a multiplier effect. Just look around and you'll see a human being in need. The most effective help we can offer, and I know this from experience, is on an individual basis. There are a thousand ways to help – a child who needs guidance, an old relative whom the family has forgotten, people in hospitals and nursing homes whom nobody visits. Not everyone is meant to venture into the sewers. The only requirement to help others is just to do it.

(Jaime Jaramillo)

THINGS TO DO

▸ Prepare a five-minute talk on the work of Jaime Jaramillo. In your talk be prepared to explain how he is very close to the ideals of the Christian Gospel.

▸ In your own words, write down the answers to these questions.

1 Give some of the reasons for children living on the streets.
2 In what parts of the world is this most usual?
3 Can you think of ways we, in the West, may be responsible? (This will be discussed later in the book.)
4 Do you think the temporary help offered by Mark and Alex is worthwhile? Give reasons for your answer.

The Spirit of the Lord is upon me,
because he has chosen me to bring
good news to the poor.
He has sent me to proclaim liberty to
the captives
and recovery of sight to the blind;
to set free the oppressed
and announce that the time has come
when the Lord will save his people.

(Luke 4:18–19)

In these words Jesus announced his manifesto, his announcement to the world that God's way – therefore his way – was about liberation. He was speaking not only about people actually behind prison bars, but about all of us. Everyone is a prisoner to something. Archbishop Desmond Tutu of South Africa shrewdly observed: 'One section of the community cannot be truly free while another is denied a share of that freedom.'

At the time he spoke, Archbishop Tutu was referring to political prisoners behind bars for claiming human rights. But his words apply to every other prison situation. A Christian would have to say: 'I am not free as long as that hit-and-run driver is serving time; as long as that murderer is locked away; as long as that girl is on remand for drug offences.' Why is this a Christian response to crime and punishment?

- Because of the responsibility Christians believe they have for another. 'No man is an island.'
- Because each human being is made in the likeness of God. Such dignity is obscured in prison situations.
- Because Christians believe God forgives every sin without retribution. Prisoners point out that human beings fail to act in the same way.

The treatment of crime is a problem for Christians. How can they show their disapproval of sin and wrongdoing and at the same time show God's forgiveness? It is possible to hate the sin and love the sinner. That is what Jesus did. But he simply said to sinners: 'Go, and sin no more.'

The Catholic response to this difficulty is expressed by organizations such as the Bourne Trust. It was founded nearly 100 years ago to 'serve prisoners and their families'. Today Trust members are professional people, e.g. counsellors, who offer support to distressed families. They work to improve visiting conditions and they encourage Catholic communities to attend Mass at prisons in order to show friendship and support. In some places Bourne Trust works alongside the St Vincent de Paul Society (see Unit 47) to rehabilitate former prisoners and their families.

Every prison in the UK has a Catholic prison chaplain, and in some places today these are women, like Clare Banyard. She took the courageous step of leaving the security of a religious teaching congregation to live alone, as a lay woman representing the Church to prisoners. She wrote recently:

I was in a dirty, airless cell in HMP Wandsworth meeting a new prisoner. As I often do in an initial encounter, I teased a little to help disperse the tension. 'We chaplains are around,' I said, 'and if we can support you in any way, do contact us… but', I added, 'I can't supply a ladder to get you over the wall!' The other man in the cramped cell, for whom I had phoned a worried mother the day before to assure her that he was all right, spontaneously chipped in, 'You are the ladder'.

Vietnamese boat people held in detention camps in Hong Kong

Prisoners have time for reflection and some of them develop new skills in communication. The following are poems and thoughts written by prisoners, at present in custody.

'God, I pray to you
To keep my family safe
And guide them on the
right path
Give them strength to
carry on
During these difficult
times
Let them learn to forgive
As you do
And be kind to others
Amen.'

(Carina)

'Tour high walls cold and bare
You look around there's no one there
A hollow voice that has no face
An echoing noise about the place.
For myself I do not mind
But heartache for my babes left behind
It's my fault, I'm to blame
But they suffer, just the same.
Lonely hours to think of my past
the shame and sorrow I have cast
Could it be but a bad dream
Not as frightening as it may seem?
I pinch myself to no avail
And accept the fact that I'm in jail.'

(Risley)

'Lord, forgive my indecision, my confusion. Help
me to think with positive thoughts so that my life
may grow and with it my love for You.'

(Charlotte)

'Oh Lord, help us to be thankful for the things
that we have and others long for.'

(Gill)

REFLECTION

Do we pray that the Holy Spirit will send us 'to bring the good news to the poor, to proclaim liberty to captives, sight to the blind and freedom to the oppressed'? To be liberated, we need to be in relationship with the God in each other, to share the message of hope and to commit ourselves to act justly, love tenderly and walk humbly with our God. Without that, we are not truly free.

(Nan Saeki, Chair, Justice and Peace Groups)

THINGS TO DO

▶ These are the reasons given for sending people to prison:
- to protect society
- for revenge – 'an eye for an eye'
- to deter others from crime
- to reform the offender.

Do you think any, or all of these, are compatible with the Christian teaching on forgiveness? Discuss in groups of four and report back to the whole class.

▶ Write short answers to the following questions:
1 What is described on these pages as Jesus' manifesto?
2 'Everyone is a prisoner to something.' Give some examples to show you have understood this.
3 Christians have a problem over the treatment of crime.
   a Explain the problem.
   b Suggest ways of tackling it.
4 'There are some crimes that cannot be forgiven.' Discuss.

And so we must begin to live again,
We of the damaged bodies
And assaulted minds.
Starting from scratch with the rubble of our lives
And picking up the dust
Of dreams once dreamt…

We, without a future,
Safe, defined, delivered
Now salute you God.
Knowing that nothing is safe,
Secure, inviolable here.
Except you,
And even that eludes our minds at times.
And we hate you
As we love you,
And our anger is as strong
As our pain,
Our grief is deep as oceans,
And our need as great as mountains...

(Anna McKenzie in *Good Friday People*, 1991)

In this poem, Anna is speaking for every wounded person; those suffering in mind and body, and their friends and family who may agonize on their behalf. She is a twentieth-century psalmist – a believer – who is not afraid to be angry with God. Many of the psalms, written years ago, express the same emotions:

How much longer will you forget
    me, Lord, For ever?
How much longer will you hide
    yourself from me?
How long must I endure trouble?
How long will sorrow fill my heart
    day and night?
How long will my enemies triumph
    over me?…
I rely on your constant love;
I will be glad, because you will rescue me.
I will sing to you, O Lord,
    because you have been good to me.

(*Psalm 13(12)*)

The greatest characteristic of people of deep faith in God is their ability to go on trusting and loving in the face of incredible grief. Some individuals even offer their personal faith and trust in God as a gift to others, by dedicating their lives to those who suffer most. The sense of service and calling is called vocation (see p. 84). Here are some Catholic lay people whose faith has touched the lives of disabled or dying people.

JEAN VANIER

Jean Vanier is a pioneer in caring for mentally disabled people. 'Caring' may be the wrong word – he lives among them and recognizes that the so-called 'normal' people are often the injured ones. Thirty years ago, after visiting a home for mentally disabled men, he invited two of them to live with him. From this beginning has grown *L'Arche* communities, 20 of them around Trosly-Breuil in France and more than 100 around the world. Assistants and people with mental disabilities live side by side, as families. The homes are not institutions. Christine McGrievy, leader of the Trosley community, explains that 'People come first, structures are only added to give the security and rhythm necessary for growth'. People who know the communities say that it is the mentally disabled people who give the most; it is the assistants who come away healed.

Life in a *L'Arche* community is rooted in shared prayer, shared work and shared responsibility. Jean Vanier has proved to everyone that it is possible to see the face of God in human suffering.

LEONARD CHESHIRE

When Lord Cheshire, VC, OM, DSO, DFC, died he received a mention in the Queen's Christmas Day message to the nation. But it was not as a war hero that he was to become famous, rather for his work over 45 years for people with physical disabilities. In 1948, he took a homeless ex-serviceman into his own home and cared for him until he died. This was the start of the Cheshire Homes. Today, there are 85 Homes in the UK, 38 Care at Home Services (CAHS) and the Cheshire Foundation is working in 50 countries.

Leonard Cheshire was a Group Captain in the RAF during the Second World War, a bomber leader and later an observer when the second atomic bomb was dropped on Nagasaki, Japan. This mission imprinted itself on his mind, and may well have

Pony-driving at the Cheshire home in Devon

Sheila Cassidy at a hospital fund-raising event

influenced his decision to work for disabled ex-soldiers. It was Arthur, his first 'resident', who led Cheshire to the Catholic Church by introducing him to Fr Clarke in Petersfield.

All his life Cheshire was restless for silence and contemplation. He even broke off a long engagement to his fiancée, Hélène, when the thought of monastic quiet attracted him. (He later married Sue Ryder.) But he resolutely looked for 'God's will' and in the end believed it was to be in helping disabled people. His life was a struggle with illness and the difficulties of developing the work, but he left the Cheshire Foundation as his memorial.

THE HOSPICE MOVEMENT

It is interesting that it is Christians – even with their belief that death is not the end of life – who have developed the hospice movement in Britain. Like Mother Teresa, who began her work caring for dying outcasts, the Anglican Cecily Saunders and the Catholic Sheila Cassidy have concentrated their love and skill on bringing comfort and relief to the dying.

Both have dedicated their lives to finding ways of easing the physical pain of dying. They use their medical knowledge to control suffering, and their Christian conviction about life after death to give people dignity and calm in their last days.

Cecily Saunders trained and worked as a nurse, then a doctor, in London, founding St Christopher's Hospice, Sydenham in 1961. Sheila Cassidy, after arrest and torture in Chile in 1975 for giving medical treatment to a revolutionary, worked for some years as Medical Director of St Luke's Hospice in Plymouth.

THINGS TO DO

▶ Research the work of the hospice movement, *L'Arche* or the Cheshire Foundation.

▶ Why do you think some people choose to go into the 'caring' professions? Do they get something out of it?

▶ It has been suggested that young people opt only to go on short-term voluntary projects because it will look good on their CV. Write about 300 words in their defence.

Only a prejudiced person would claim to be without bias, for the fact is we are all prejudiced in some way or other. The word itself means to prejudge, that is, we judge another without having either knowledge or experience.

(*How the Churches Decide*)

The Catholic Church, like all the Christian Churches, is speaking out today on many issues where prejudice has embittered situations for centuries. It is quite clear that the Churches are not without blame; for they themselves have acted with discrimination and prejudice over the centuries.

In 1994, Catholic bishops asked forgiveness of the Central American Indians for the imperialistic way they treated them in the past. When Pope John Paul II was on a visit to Peru, the Tupac Indians handed him a letter:

We the Indians of the Andes and America, have decided to take the opportunity of this visit by the Pope to return to him his Bible. In five centuries it has brought us neither love, nor peace, nor justice. Please take your Bible back, and return it to our oppressors. It is they, rather than we, who have need of its moral precepts.

This is a sad reflection on the failure of the Catholic Church. Some would say there are other failures – over women in the Church, over attitudes to the Jews, over homosexuality.

On the positive side, Catholics can point to consistent Catholic teaching that all people, created in God's image, are equal in his sight. Every Catholic secondary school probably has a poster of Martin Luther King with his words:

I have a dream that one day this nation will rise up and live out the true meaning of its creed: 'We hold these truths to be self-evident; that all men are created equal.'

PREJUDICE: the unfair attitude we take to others before we have even got to know them.

STEREOTYPES: the inaccurate, false images we build in our minds of groups of people.

DISCRIMINATION: the way we treat some people unfavourably and so cause them suffering.

People suffer prejudice and discrimination on many grounds: race, colour, sex, age, social group. The difficulty is that prejudices become so rooted in society that people can be quite ignorant of what they are doing to others. Racism, for example, is deeply ingrained in our history, and has become institutionalized, so that as a result non-white people are often at a disadvantage when looking for jobs or good housing.

There is not the space in this book to look at prejudice in any depth; other textbooks do this more fully. Here we will simply consider the position of the Catholic Church. The position is ambiguous (unclear). This is hardly surprising since all of us act with ambiguity in our relationships with others. White parents will easily disown any discrimination against minority groups – until their daughter wants to marry into a West Indian family! Or they may claim that they are totally free of prejudice until their son reveals to them that he is gay. The Church professes to be open to all, with no discrimination, yet Church history shows that it does not always live up to the fine ideal.

The Church bases its teaching first and foremost on the example of Jesus, who broke through all the prejudiced barriers of his day: he mixed with Samaritans, sinners, women and social outcasts, such as tax gatherers.

The early Church had learnt from Jesus:

He created all races of mankind and made them live throughout the whole earth.

(*Acts 17:26*)

So there is no difference between Jews and Gentiles, between slaves and free men, between men and women; you are all one in union with Christ Jesus.

(Galatians 3:28)

You will be doing the right thing if you obey the law of the Kingdom, which is found in the Scripture, 'Love your neighbour as you love yourself.' But if you treat people according to their outward appearance, you are guilty of sin.

(James 2:8–9)

The Catholic Church today preaches the same message:

Truth calls for the elimination of every trace of racial discrimination, and the consequent recognition of the inviolable principle that all states are by nature equal in dignity.

(Pacem in Terris 86)

With respect to the fundamental rights of the person, every type of discrimination, whether social or cultural, whether based on sex, race, colour, social condition, language or religion, is to be overcome and eradicated as contrary to God's intent.

(Gaudium et Spes 29:1)

It is not just a question of fighting wretched conditions. It involves building a human community where people can live truly human lives, free from discrimination on account of race, religion or nationality, free from servitude to others.

(Populorum Progressio 47)

In 1989 the Catholic Church published a statement on *The Church and Racism*. It reflected on the (then) institutionalized racism of South Africa, the position of aboriginal peoples, religious minorities, of different ethnic groups, refugees and immigrants, as well as those affected by social and spontaneous racism, and especially anti-Semitism (racism against Jews). The document outlined three responses:

1   Diversity should be accepted and respected as something positive, not negative.

2   Charity and justice require that everyone should have dignified living conditions to allow them to recognize each other as brothers and sisters.
3   This, in turn, should lead to solidarity between all races.

THINGS TO DO

▶ The 1989 document recognizes that the role of schools is vital in promoting good racial harmony. Discuss this in groups. Each group should offer one practical idea that could be adopted in your school.

▶ Write out the list of discriminations in the *Gaudium et Spes* quotation. In groups of four, discuss each one in relation to the Catholic Church itself. How far has the Church managed to free itself from discrimination?

▶ Read the reflection below.

1   Write a letter to the press criticizing or supporting the government's decision never to release Myra Hindley. Explain the reasons for your opinion.

2   How free of prejudice have the media been on this matter?

REFLECTION

Myra Hindley has been in prison for nearly 30 years for her part in the Moors child murders. Public opinion still runs high on her case. There is a small group of campaigners, led by Lord Longford, who plead for her release, on the grounds she has changed into a remorseful, well-informed and religious woman. They accuse even the parole board of prejudice in this case. The press still fuel public outrage against Myra Hindley and say she should never be released. Some call for the return of the death penalty for her.

In December 1994 the Home Office decided that she should never be set free.

On Sunday morning Sean and his family go to Mass. After the opening prayers they all stand to 'greet the Gospel'. The Bible is carried in solemn procession, escorted by candle-bearers and greeted with alleluias. At the lectern, the priest or deacon may bless the book with **incense**. Sean's family join in the acclamation 'Glory to you, Lord' as the reading is announced, and finally in the response, 'Praise to you, Lord Jesus Christ', when the reading is finished and the reader kisses the text. It is as though Christ himself is present in the reading.

The next day Sean joins his RE class for a study of the Gospel for his GCSE. The same Bible is used, open on the desks, but this time texts are analysed and discussed, even critically; it is not unlike researching literature in English lessons.

On Sunday, the Bible was seen as the Word of God. On Monday, it was thought of as a piece of human literature. Is there any contradiction here? Together with other Christians, the Catholic Church sees the Bible as both Word of God and words of humans. God's activity never excludes human activity. How else could God act other than through human beings? The Bible is the supreme example of this.

Bible is a Greek word meaning 'book'. For Christians, it is the most important of all books. They call it their *Scripture*, which is Latin for 'sacred writings'. It was written over many years by different people and is, in fact, composed of 60 or 70 books (different groups number them differently).

But as Christians hear God speaking to them through the variety of writings (poetry, history, law, stories) they regard it as one holy book. Bound as a single work, it falls into two distinct parts – the **Old Testament** and the **New Testament** – because it records the testaments or agreements by which God has bound himself to his people. God speaks through these pages of the Bible, and Christians say 'Amen' (I agree to that).

THE OLD TESTAMENT

These books tell the story of the Jewish people and are part of their sacred writings. The story is based on the contract the people of Israel believe God made with them, through their leader Moses. The 40 or so books are divided into three sections, which Jews call The Law, The Prophets and The Holy Writings.

The Christian Church has adopted the Jewish Scriptures because they were the Word of God for Jesus. Without these writings, Jesus could never be understood.

THE CANON OF THE BIBLE

The list of books in the Bible is known as the Canon which means 'rule'. Believers accept that these books rule their lives. The Jews did not all agree on which books should form their canon. Two canons resulted: a proto (or first) canon of 38 books accepted by Palestinian Jews, and a deutero (or second) canon of 45 books accepted by the later community of dispersed Jews, living in the Greek world.

The Christian Church adopted the longer deutero canon, which included: *Baruch, Judith, Tobit, Ecclesiasticus, Wisdom, I Maccabees* and *II Maccabees*. The Catholic Bible still includes these seven books, but the Protestant reformers omitted them from their Bibles and referred to them as Apocrypha.

The RE class study Luke's Gospel for their GCSE

THE NEW TESTAMENT

This is the second part of the Bible for Christians. It tells the story of the testament or covenant Christians believe God made with them through Jesus. It consists of 27 books, which fall into the following groups.

The Synoptic Gospels

Synoptic means 'look alike'. Gospel means 'good news'. These are three parallel interpretations of the life and death of Jesus as good news for everyone:

- *Matthew*
- *Mark*
- *Luke.*

The Pauline books

Luke expanded his Gospel into a second volume, to tell the work of Paul. The epistles (letters) he wrote follow:

- *Acts of the Apostles*
- *Romans*

- *1 Corinthians*
- *2 Corinthians*
- *Galatians*
- *Ephesians*
- *Philippians*
- *Colossians*
- *1 Thessalonians*
- *2 Thessalonians*
- *1 Timothy*
- *2 Timothy*
- *Titus*
- *Philemon*
- *Hebrews.*

The General Epistles

Letters written by other early Christian leaders:

- *James*
- *1 Peter*
- *2 Peter*
- *Jude.*

The Johannine books

The good news told by John and his followers:

- *John's Gospel*
- *3 Epistles of John*
- *Revelation.*

St Paul the Apostle and writer of letters to the early Church

THINGS TO DO

▶ Write down the meaning of the following words:

- Bible
- Scripture
- Amen
- Testament
- Canon
- Proto-canon
- Deutero-canon
- Apocrypha
- Covenant
- Synoptic
- Epistle.

Until recently most Catholics attached little importance to the Bible. It was as if all they needed to know was in the Catechism and Church documents.

This negative attitude dates back to the sixteenth century, when Protestants appealed to the Bible against the Church, and the counter-emphasis on Church tradition (see p. 82) gave the impression that the Bible, especially when privately interpreted, was a dangerous book. Catholics read it less and less, especially when 100 years ago Popes Leo XIII and Pius X wrote very discouragingly about the work of biblical scholars. One Jesuit priest tells how little he studied the Bible during his priestly training:

> If my memory serves me well, we were never directly encouraged to read the Bible, not even the New Testament; whereas time was specifically allocated to certain spiritual writers renowned for their views on religious discipline.

> (A Patrick Purnell, *Our Faith Story*)

A total change began to take place about 50 years ago. In 1943 Pope Pius XII gave his blessing to new methods of Bible study in a papal document *Divino Afflante Spiritu* ('Under the Inspiration of God's Spirit'). This was reinforced 20 years later in the Vatican Council Document *Dei Verbum* ('Word of God'), which urges Catholics to become more familiar with the Bible.

IS THE BIBLE TRUE?

> The things that you're liable
> To read in the Bible
> They ain't necessarily so.

> (George Gershwin, *Porgy and Bess*)

When people ask, 'Is the Bible true?' they usually mean should it be taken literally? The answer is that some of it is and some is not, depending on the way in which the authors meant their words to be understood. That Jesus had a mother called Mary is obviously meant literally – St Luke probably knew her personally. That the world as we know it came into being over six days is obviously not meant literally – the author of the first chapter of *Genesis* had no idea of the origins of the world discovered by modern science; but he could still express, in a fine piece of poetry, his faith in a God 'who's got the whole world in his hands'.

The study of history and archaeology, of the background of the Bible authors – of their ideas, their purpose, their styles of writing (history, legend, folklore, parables, etc.) – is called *exegesis*, and is essential for understanding what the Bible is saying and what it does not say. Even the Gospels are not simply a biography of someone in the past, but a profession of faith in what Jesus means to the author (and to the reader) now. 'What does it mean?' is the question to ask, not 'What really happened?' Sometimes we can no longer tell.

THE CATHOLIC APPROACH TO INTERPRETING THE BIBLE

Times have changed. Catholics were once deeply suspicious of Protestant scholars. Today, they work together, and Protestants and Jews such as Evans, Hooker, Nineham and Vermes both respect and are respected by Catholics such as Brown, Fitzmyer, McKenzie and Murphy O'Connor. New guidelines issued by Rome's Pontifical Biblical Commission in 1994 (*The Interpretation of the Bible in the Church*) strongly support the scholars who search for a new understanding of Bible texts. Cardinal Ratzinger writes in the preface:

> The study of the Bible is never finished; each age must in its own way newly seek to understand the sacred books.

There are three particularly interesting sections in this new document:

1 The text must be 'actualized', so that we know what the Bible means today. This can of course be abused: the document points out that the Bible has sometimes been exploited to justify racism, anti-semitism and sexism. Yet it remains important that the Bible speaks to Christians today and not only to people in the past.
2 The document comments: 'A particular cause for satisfaction in our time is the growing number of women exegetes; they frequently contribute new and penetrating insights and rediscover features which had been forgotten.'
3 There is a brisk attack on Christian fundamentalism. Fundamentalists treat the biblical text as though it had been dictated word for word by the Spirit and make no allowance for the individuality of the human authors.

To understand how the Bible is used by Catholics today consider the following example. *Luke 9:10–17* tells the story of the feeding of the five thousand. There was a time when no one dreamt of taking this text as anything other than a blow-by-blow account of what happened. Being God, Jesus could do anything, even the impossible. Miracles like this simply backed up claims Jesus made for himself.

Preachers might link this bread story with the bread of the Eucharist, where Jesus continues to exercise the same almighty power over nature.

Scholars, however, would wish to look more deeply into the origins of the story, which (like many of Luke's stories) is based on the Old Testament. Luke sees Jesus as the prophet Elisha returned to life (see *2 Kings 4:42–4*), just as earlier he had seen him as a reincarnation of Elijah bringing the dead back to life, (compare *Luke 7:15* with *1 Kings 17:23*). All this means that the actual historical event in the life of Jesus ('what really happened') can no longer be recovered. What we know is that those who lived with Jesus represented him as the one without whom they could die of hunger on their journey through life.

When a Christian 'actualizes' this text it means asking the question: 'Is the same true for me?'

THINGS TO DO

▶ Briefly explain what types of literature are found in the Bible.

▶ Explain how the Bible is used in Catholic worship.

▶ What is meant by exegesis?

▶ Christians call the Bible 'The Word of God in human words'. What do they mean?

▶ How far can the Bible be taken literally? Give reasons for your answer.

The Bible story of Jonah, taken from an illuminated Bible from Ranworth church in Norfolk

After many years of discussion, and in spite of some strong disagreement, the Anglican Church recently decided to ordain women as well as men to the priesthood. The first women were ordained in 1994. On what authority? How do the Churches make decisions on controversial matters?

The answer is that different denominations act in different ways. But they all agree that no one can make up the rules as they go along. Three factors have to be taken into account.

1 SCRIPTURE

All Christians accept the Bible as the rule (canon) by which they will measure things. They regard the Bible as a unique and unchangeable expression of the way in which God has made himself known, first in the history of the Jewish people, and then in the life of Jesus. 'Does it accord with Scripture?' is one of the questions which must be asked?

2 TRADITION

There are, however, many matters on which the Bible can give no firm answer. It needs interpreting, because it is only a written form of something much wider, the Church's tradition.

Tradition means 'what is handed on, from one generation to another' – and what Christians have handed on down the centuries is not only a book, but a whole way of life. Jesus did not say, 'Write a book about me.' He said, 'Follow me, live like me.' So the Church 'in her teaching, her life and worship, perpetuates and hands on [tradition] to all generations all that she herself is, and all she believes.' (*Dei Verbum 8*)

Tradition is the Church living out its understanding of Christ. All Christians, of all denominations, share this sense of tradition, and acknowledge that they will need to take account of what their Christian ancestors (the Church Fathers, the Saints, the theologians) have said when they make decisions.

3 EXPERIENCE AND REASON

Applying the Bible and Christian tradition to new circumstances is rarely a straightforward business. People will also need to use their own power of reasoning (which is as much God's gift as the Bible is), their own experience, their own judgement and their own conscience, in order to reach a responsible conclusion. No one can do believing for someone else: you have to do it yourself.

Anglican women deacons were first ordained priests in 1994

The process of decision-making may be summed up as follows:

The Catholic community comes to an understanding of new and contemporary problems by an appreciation of all sources of God's self-revelation:

1 the insight of the Scriptures;

2 the tradition of the Church, the way the Fathers of the Church have reflected on the Scriptures in their own context and history;

3 the wisdom of the scholastic philosophers, who build up a coherent picture relating the Scriptures to human life and thought;

4 the on-going theological reflection in different parts of the Church in different historical contexts;

5 the contemporary experience of the people of God struggling to live out their faith in justice.

(How the Churches Decide)

THE MAGISTERIUM

The Latin word *magister* means 'teacher'. **Magisterium** is the word used for the teaching role that the Church is conscious of possessing in the light of Christ's command:

'Go and preach, the Kingdom of heaven is near.' (Matthew 10:7)
'What you have heard in private you must announce from the housetops.' (Matthew 10:27)
'Going therefore, teach ye all nations' (Matthew 28:19, Douay Version)
'Whoever listens to you listens to me.' (Luke 10:16)

This teaching role, of course, belongs to all Christians: without even intending to, they will preach Christ to others by their Christian way of life. It is this responsibility of the whole community that is stressed by those who see the Church as a series of circles rather than as a pyramid (see p. 90).

In the Catholic Catechism the word *magisterium* is more normally used of the bishops exercising their official role as teachers of the Christian faith. This day-to-day teaching is called the 'ordinary *magisterium*'. It becomes 'extraordinary' when they solemnly gather together in council (as they did in thousands at Vatican II in 1963–5) in order to discuss and formulate what Christians believe; or when the Pope speaks on behalf of his brother bishops explicitly and solemnly to define a point of faith or morals for the whole Church. In such rare cases, Catholics believe, the providence of God will continue to preserve the Church from error in handing on the Word of God.

Yet even on issues where the official teaching of the Catholic Church seems to have said the last word (as on the ordination of women or the celibacy of priests), it is quite normal for discussion to continue, not only among ordinary people, but among scholars and theologians. This means that it is not always easy to answer the question, 'What does the Catholic Church say on x?' (Unless one were to say that these people do not form part of the Church!)

Such disagreements can dishearten some Catholics, especially younger ones. But the Church has always held together different theologies and opinions. Some would say this is a weakness. Others regard it as a strength. St Paul said that God's power is shown in weakness. Perhaps this is the reason that the number of Catholics continues to grow in spite of disagreements and disappointments.

THINGS TO DO

▶ Write short notes about the following:

● Scripture

● Tradition

● Experience and tradition

● The *magisterium*.

A news report from Damascus, Syria, appeared in a British newspaper under the headline 'Myrna and the oil: an everyday miracle'.

The report described Myrna Nazzour, a young woman who has visions of Our Lady and whose hands mysteriously ooze oil. The journalist, without any sentimentality, went to investigate the 'phenomenon'. The account she wrote is remarkable for its dignity.

Myrna and her husband, in the early days of their marriage, found a cheap picture of Mary that stood by their bedside, oozing oil. Then a terrified Myrna found oil coming from her hands. Three times she developed *stigmata* – wounds in her head, hands, feet and side, which bled. This was followed by visions of Our Lady who asked that Christians pray for peace and unity.

Was the journalist expecting to find a strange, rather eccentric woman, perhaps a recluse, when she met Myrna? She describes, in fact, an ordinary, kind, young wife and mother who goes about her daily tasks with no fuss. She noticed, too, that Myrna and her husband live in great simplicity and that their lives are spent quietly serving others, visiting the sick and dying, listening to people's problems. Her husband says of her: 'She has the cleanest heart I have ever known.'

When the journalist inquired further from Church authority about the case, she was told: 'The best evidence for the truth of the story was the Nazzours' own lives, especially the husband's, who had been an ordinary man of the world. Neither of them were religious at all – but now they live a life of prayer. You could possibly fake that for a few months, but not for 12 years.'

RELIGIOUS EXPERIENCE

What is happening here? Myrna Nazzour had an extraordinary religious experience which has affected her physically. It is clear that the experience spoke to her with enormous authority. It dramatically changed her life; and in turn is having an influence on many others.

Most people who claim to have a religious experience do not have any outward proof of it to show to others, in the way Myrna had. But there are many people who have a moment of deep awareness of something greater touching their lives than can be seen or recognized outwardly. For example, they say:

- 'I suddenly knew what I had to do.'

- 'I went to the concert, and came out a changed person.'

- 'I went reluctantly to the Kintbury retreat, but it was a wonderful experience at a depth I never knew existed. I have to go back there.'

Personal experiences which touch on the reality that Christians call God speak with far greater authority to the individuals than anything else. Poets manage to capture the experience in words, such as Wordsworth in his poem 'Tintern Abbey'. The seventeenth-century philosopher Blaise Pascal recorded his experience on paper which was found sewn into his clothing after his death:

From about half past ten in the evening to about half an hour after midnight.
Fire.
God of Abraham, God of Isaac, God of Jacob.
Not the God of philosophers and scholars.
Absolute Certainty. Beyond reason. Joy. Peace.
Forgetfulness of the world and everything but God.
The world has not known thee, but I have known thee.
Joy! Joy! Joy! Tears of joy!

VOCATION

When Christians have such religious experiences, it is not unusual for them to make a lasting decision about their future lives. The experience speaks with such authority that they opt to build their lives on it. The Gospel takes on a new meaning. The Catholic National Religious Vocation Centre has described this sense of calling, known as **vocation**, in these words:

In the New Testament Jesus called his followers to build the Kingdom of God by way of discipleship, by living the Gospel values; later on some of Jesus' followers were calling others to serve the Church, to minister to one another preaching, teaching or healing. All were called to follow Jesus on the way to the Father.

Each one of us has been given a similar call to follow the Lord and to use our gifts and talents for each other in making God's Kingdom of love, truth, peace and justice, present on earth in our time.

We are called to follow Christ in various ways – as married or single persons, as priests or religious.

Sister Maureen (right) happy on the occasion of her final Profession of Vows

TWO CHRISTIANS WITH A SENSE OF MISSION

Sean Devereux is the perfect example of a young Catholic man who grew up with a sense of vocation, as natural to him as breathing air. From his family, his parish and his Catholic school he absorbed the Gospel, especially the call to justice for all people. He left the comfort of England and a PE teaching post for the discomfort of North Africa and later of war-torn Mogadishu. There, working for the United Nations, he was martyred, for his uncompromising search for justice for the poor.

Sister Maureen MacKenzie is a Notre Dame nun who teaches profoundly disabled children at a Clydebank school. She did not have a dramatic religious experience to lead her to a convent; just a nagging awareness that she should do more with her life. The thought began when she was at university, but she dismissed it at first because she loved sport, had a boyfriend and enjoyed socializing. It was working in Nigeria with the sisters that convinced her of the call to religious life.

THINGS TO DO

▶ Find out more about people like Sean Devereux and Sr Maureen. Talk to people in your school who have a sense of vocation: a teacher, the school chaplain (if you have one).

▶ Write 250 words describing to an unbeliever how religious experience is a reality to many people.

▶ Design a poster to attract new members to a religious order.

▶ Read the following passages in the Bible. List the common themes you find in them:

Genesis 12:1–4 (Abraham)
1 Samuel 3:1–10 (Samuel)
Exodus 3:1–14 (Moses)
Jeremiah 1:4–10 (Jeremiah)
Isaiah 6:1–8 (Isaiah)
Luke 1:26–38 (Mary)
Matthew 4:18–22 (Apostles)
Luke 18:18–25 (Young Man)
Acts 9:1–19 (Paul)

What would you do with this money found on the school drive?

You see a £5 note on the school drive. What do you do? Three people gave these answers:

- 'I'd put it in my pocket. People should be more careful. Finders, keepers, I say.' (John)
- 'If no one saw me I'd probably keep it – £5 isn't much these days. Whoever lost it mightn't even notice.' (Susan)
- 'I'd take it to the school office and hand it in.' (Sam)

We can say that Sam 'had a conscience'. What is a conscience? It is certainly powerful enough to make Sam act honestly and ignore the temptation to act like Susan and John.

Conscience, according to the Catholic Church, is the voice of God speaking in the individual.

◇

Deep within his conscience man discovers a law which he has not laid upon himself but which he must obey. Its voice, ever calling him to love and to do what is good and to avoid evil, sounds in his heart at the right moment... For man has in his heart a law inscribed by God...His conscience is man's most secret core and his sanctuary. There he is alone with God whose voice echoes in his depths.

(*Gaudium et Spes 16*)

It is unlikely that Sam was conscious of listening to the voice of God when he returned the money. He probably would say: 'I just knew it was the right thing to do.' Many people, not necessarily religious, have this sense of moral rightness. It is usually learnt from parents or from sensitive teaching about the rights of others. It is picked up in a general environment of community awareness. Some people today believe that Britain has become so materialistic that conscience is being stifled and young people are losing the sense of rightness that Sam showed.

The Catholic Church places a strong emphasis on the responsibility of parents and teachers to develop the conscience of young children, and on individuals to develop their own conscience.

A well-formed conscience is upright and truthful. It formulates its judgements according to reason, in conformity with the true good willed by the wisdom of the Creator. Everyone must avail himself of the means to form his conscience.

(*Catechism of the Catholic Church*, No. 1798)

Conscience can demand action. The story of *Franz Jägerstätter* is a striking example of the powerful authority conscience can have. During the Second World War, Franz, a Catholic farmer in Austria, refused to fight in Hitler's army. He was told by all the authorities, including priests and bishops, that he had a duty to obey the call to fight for his country. The greatest pressure was put on him to fight to defend his own wife and children. 'Again and again, people stress the obligations of conscience as they concern my wife and children. But I cannot believe that, just because one has a wife and children, he is free to offend God by lying.' He was executed on 9 August 1943 for obeying his own conscience.

THINGS TO DO

▶ Write out a definition of conscience.

▶ Write out a conversation between Susan and Sam over the £5 note incident.

▶ The Catechism says: 'Everyone must avail himself of the means to form his conscience.' What are these means?

▶ Do you agree with those who think that the conscientious Sam (p. 86) is the exception in Britain today? Would all your class agree?

▶ What would you do in these situations?

● You see one of your year group cheating in an important exam.

● A friend confides in you that she is getting hooked on smoking and dare not tell her parents. She can't afford her habit and has stolen from them.

● One of your family is bringing home pieces of equipment from his work place. You suspect that he is stealing them.

● You have a collection of school library books and text books at home. You are embarrassed to return them.

Compare answers across the class and display the results. Try to find out the reasons for the answers people gave.

CLASS DEBATE

Hold a class debate on:

This house believes that conscience is not the voice of God but the voice of your parents.

Two people should propose the motion and two people should oppose it.

SURVEY

When you have read Part 6, carry out a survey on religious authority.

1 Each member of the class should interview three Christians for homework. They should ask them on what or whose authority they believe in God:

a the Bible
b the Church's teaching
c their own experience
d their conscience
e a combination of some of the above
f a combination of all of the above.

2 In class collect all the replies and present the results in a graphic display.
3 Discuss the results and come to some conclusion about them. Write a summary of this.

Members of the Catholic Church are aware of two ways in which its organization can be described. The first way is the more traditional. It starts with the Pope, as leader, at the top. This model is shared by the Orthodox Christians, but not by the Reformed Churches. A second model starting from below, with the community itself, is discussed in the next unit.

THE POPE

The Pope lives in the Vatican, a state in its own right, in the centre of Rome, Italy. He lives there because it is the burial place of Peter, the Apostle. The Pope leads the Roman Catholic Church by his teaching, often published in encyclical letters, but more usually preached in Rome or when travelling the world. He is assisted by his bishops, and he regularly calls representatives of them to Synod meetings to discuss important issues.

Occasionally, Popes call General Councils when all bishops must attend and documents or decrees are produced which have to be accepted by the whole Church. The Pope is assisted by committees, many based in Rome, called the Curia. International Commissions advise the Pope on various issues.

Some important documents from Popes or Councils

- *Mater et Magistra* – John XXIII
- *Pacem in Terris* – John XXIII
- *Gaudium et Spes* – Vatican II
- *Lumen Gentium* – Vatican II
- *Populorum Progressio* – Paul VI
- *Justice in the World* – Synod, 1971
- *Redemptor Hominis* – John Paul II
- *Veritatis Splendor* – John Paul II
- *Catechism of the Catholic Church*, 1994

Pope John Paul II, at a ceremony in Rome

THE CARDINALS

The Pope selects an international team (college) of close advisers with the title, Cardinal. It is they who gather in Rome, in the Sistine Chapel, to elect the new Pope. The English Cardinal adviser is Basil Hume, who was formerly the Benedictine Abbot of Ampleforth. In Scotland, Thomas Winning was appointed Cardinal in 1994.

THE BISHOPS

The Catholic Church is divided into hundreds of provinces, each under an archbishop, and then into thousands of dioceses, each under a **bishop**. Each country has a Bishops' Conference, where national issues are debated and local commissions set up. Overall responsibility for the national Catholic Church rests with this Conference.

THE PRIESTS AND DEACONS

Bishops are assisted in their work by priests. A diocese is divided up into smaller units, called parishes. This local community is led in worship, and taught in sermons, by priests. Large parishes appoint male **deacons**, some married, to assist the priests.

THE LAITY

The remaining Church members are called lay people, or laity. Today, a few important tasks are being given to them in the running of the diocese. Many of these roles are filled by nuns: catechetical centre workers, members of national commissions and chaplains to universities or prisons. Lay people can become more involved by being members of the parish or diocesan council, or by organizing parish activities and groups.

THE CATHOLIC CHURCH IN BRITAIN

Cardinals and bishops gather for a celebration at St John's Roman Catholic Cathedral in Norwich

During the sixteenth-century Reformation, the formal structure of the Catholic Church ceased to exist in England. It was restored in 1850. The Scottish Church's formal structure ceased in the early seventeenth century and was restored in 1878. Catholicism never completely disappeared, however, especially as Irish immigrants arrived in England in the nineteenth century.

In the 1840s there was a major conversion to the Catholic Church from the Anglican Church, led by John Henry Newman, later a cardinal. Some people anticipate a similar movement of Anglicans to the Roman Church in the next few years, following the ordination of Anglican women priests.

Structure

There are seven Catholic provinces in Great Britain, and 30 dioceses. Scotland, Ireland and England each have a cardinal. The Catholic Church in England and Wales has a Bishop's Conference, whose members include diocesan bishops, a bishop of the armed forces, and the Apostolic Exarch of the Ukrainians in Britain. The Conference is divided into five departments with different responsibilities.

There is a separate Bishops' Conference in Scotland and an Irish Episcopal Conference which covers the whole of Ireland.

In England alone, there are 2800 Roman Catholic parishes which serve about one tenth of the population. Parishes have no inherited wealth; the diocese administers funds on behalf of the parishes. There are about 6300 Catholic priests in Britain today.

REFLECTIONS

'I am delighted to be part of such a highly structured Church. I am happy to know that the Pope is in charge and tells me what to do.'

(Agnes, aged 63)

'I feel a nothing in my parish, just a silent voice, with no influence because I am a woman and young.'

(Hannah, aged 16)

'I have a certain pride in being part of the hierarchical structure of the Catholic Church. I have a sense of "getting things done" when I have been at a Commission meeting.'

(Fr Luke, aged 40)

'I wish I could have more say in how our Church is run. I have much more responsibility in my professional job than I could ever have as a lay man in the Church.'

(Thomas, aged 40)

THINGS TO DO

▶ The four reflections are actual quotes from Catholics. Do you think they are typical or representative of how others feel?

▶ Imagine you are Hannah (or Henry) aged 16. Write a letter to your bishop suggesting ways you would like the Church to listen to you.

▶ Some other Christians envy the way the Pope has firm control over the Catholic Church. What reasons do you think they have for feeling this way?

A DIFFERENT MODEL OF THE CHURCH

The model of the Church bequeathed us by the Council of Trent was of a hierarchical Church... a pyramidical structure with the Pope at its peak. At the base were the laity, the recipients of authority which always passed from top to bottom. At the Second Vatican Council (1963–5) the world's bishops rejected [this model]. There had been a change of thinking going on in the Church, from conceiving herself as a hierarchical society to seeing herself as a COMMUNITY; from a pyramid to a circle.

(Adrian Smith, *Tomorrow's Parish*, 1983)

The last unit described the hierarchical model of the Church as a pyramid with the laity as the base. In that model, the laity look (and feel) depressed by the sheer weight of authority above them. This model has been accepted for so many centuries in Europe that it is very difficult to think of the Church in any other way. But new thinking has come from countries exhausted by poverty and injustice. Forty years ago a movement started in Brazil which has begun to give a new direction to the Catholic Church; today it is known as the Movement for Basic Christian Communities.

It was this experience from Brazil that influenced the Vatican Council bishops who called for a return to the early practice of forming 'Church' around small communities. Thousands of such poor communities already existed in Third World Catholic countries. Instead of dismissing them as worthless, they could be the foundation stones of a renewed Church.

A BBC schools programme, *Christianity in Today's World*, showed how one of these basic communities has changed the lives of the people who live in Nova Iguaçu, a slum area of Rio. Although Brazil has the potential to be a very rich nation, 50 per cent of its inhabitants live in absolute poverty. In Rio there are 8 million street children. Eighty per cent of Brazilians are Roman Catholics.

In the programme, a young woman, Marlucia, described her basic community.

'We meet to discuss what we need to do in order to work to produce a better reality of our lives. We have a lot of love and affection for each other. I believe this [new Church] means the individual's

A woman leads this Brazilian base community in prayer and Bible study

fight for a better tomorrow. Fighting with love, thinking of Christ, but it is a way for the individual to struggle in his day-to-day life and to improve it.'

The people meet in groups and discuss the immediate problems in the locality – blocked-up drains that have closed the school, open sewers, impossible roads, etc. They turn to the Gospels and look for encouragement from the example and words of Jesus. They pray together, and they decide what practical steps they should take. Fr Tony Sheridan, an Irish priest who works at Nova Iguaçu, says: 'We discuss our lives in relationship to our Faith. We start with the facts of life, feelings, and then we ask what Christ would do?'

This new model for the Church arises out of a different way of looking at God's relationship to people. It is called **Liberation Theology** (see Unit 45).

THINGS TO DO

Answer the following questions:

▶ What is meant by a hierarchical structure in the Church?

▶ What is a basic Christian community?

▶ Why does Adrian Smith describe one model of the Church as a pyramid and one as a circle?

▶ Do you think it would be a good idea to have basic communities in this country? Are they necessary? Would they work?

REFLECTIONS

It is exciting being a new form of Church. It isn't a different Church. It's still the same old, 2000-year-old Catholic Church, but it is a different way of expressing itself. There is a joy about that, and it is spreading to other parts of the world.

(Fr Tony Sheridan)

What we see today in Latin America is a new model of the Church. Don't fall into the error of thinking there is now a new popular Church in Latin America. There isn't. What we have found is the Christian Church founded by Christ, but it is a new way of being that Church in the World.

(Sr Pamela Hussey HCJ from a talk given at the Grail Centre)

Hope is the last thing that will go. I fight for it. My group fights for it. My Church fights for it.

(Maria José, Brazil)

The poor are the teachers, according to a basic principle of liberation theology. What do they teach me, when the gap between my technology, knowledge, money, and power and theirs is unbridgeable? How have they converted me, what have they given me?…From them I learn their hope, their toughness, their anger, and their patience. I learn a better theology in which God is not Lord-over-us but Strength-in-us. In which the miracles of Jesus are not distinguished from ours. I learn trust in the people of God. I begin to hunger and thirst after righteousness.

(Dorothee Soelle, *Celebrating Resistance*, 1993)

Liberation theology is the attempt to practise faith in situations of political, economic and social injustice. It poses a challenge to Christians worldwide because it demands change. It seeks the ultimate liberation of both rich and poor.

(Christian Aid statement)

Some Christians see their faith as totally spiritual, and as having nothing to do with the problems of this world. Liberation Theology challenges this idea, and in doing so arouses the admiration of some Christians, and the anxiety of others.

BACKGROUND

The new theology emerged in the 1960s when the Catholic Church was re-examining itself at the time of the Vatican Council. The new thinking began with the people and their needs. There has always been a tradition in the Church of service to the poor. (Some have called the Church's social teaching, 'The best kept secret in the Roman Catholic Church'.) But this was new; a determined move to re-adjust values. In 1968 at a Conference of Bishops in Medellin, Colombia, the Church spoke of taking an 'option for the poor'. The bishops committed themselves to work for liberation of the people from injustice, violence and poverty, and they renewed that commitment at Puebla in 1979. The movement has developed ever since and embraces other Christians, like those in South Africa, who produced an outspoken document called *Kairos* in 1985.

The newer model for Church community began in the shanty towns, like this one in Rio de Janeiro

THE LIBERATION THEOLOGY CHURCH

Many Church leaders cut their close links with the rich and powerful of their countries, especially governments, in order to stand alongside their poor people. The basic communities began to replace traditional local churches. The people became more assertive and active as they became aware of their own power to help themselves. ('Conscientization' is the word used to describe this process of awareness.) But not everyone responded in the same way to their problems. Here are possible reactions to injustice and poverty.

1 Acceptance of the situation

Some Christians still think that whatever happens to them is 'God's will'. They believe any rebellion against unjust government is not in keeping with the Gospel. 'Everyone must obey the state authorities because no authority exists without God's permission.' (*Romans 13:1*). 'Render to Caesar the things that are Caesar's' (*Matthew 22:21*).

2 Non-violent, quiet action

It is possible to protest against injustices in a persistent but non-aggressive way. Many people write complaints even to presidents. When US President Reagan offered humanitarian aid to the Baptist Church in Nicaragua following mass destruction by the Contra forces, they quietly refused it. His government was, at the same time, funding the Contra forces.

3 Social and political action

Some Christians, encouraged by the Church, take leading roles in social reform. President Nelson Mandela of South Africa thanked the Christians for their part in wearing down the leaders of the old apartheid regime. In Central America, political action (speeches, rallies, marches and demands for social reforms) is condemned as subversive by the government. Christians are persecuted and killed. In El Salvador many have been martyred, including Archbishop Romero, nuns, Jesuit priests and thousands of laity.

4 Counterviolence

Some Christians believe that gross injustice inflicted on the poor is so violent that lesser violence is justified in attempting to topple a violent regime.

This aspect of the liberation movement has been condemned by Rome.

Only by revolution, by changing the concrete conditions of our country, can we enable men to practise love for each other.

With these words, Fr Camillo Torres, a Colombian priest, joined a guerrilla movement to fight the government. He was killed.

REFLECTIONS

The poverty of the poor is not a summons to alleviate their plight with acts of generosity, but rather a compelling obligation to fashion an entirely different social order.

(Leading Liberation theologian, Gustavo Gutierrez)

The Catholic who is not a revolutionary is living in mortal sin.

(Camillo Torres)

The Church and the Jesuits have made an option for the poor. This is the option Jesus made; the option the prophets like Isaiah and Micah made. That doesn't make the Church Communist. That makes the Church simply Christian.

(Fr Jon Sobrino SJ, speaking on television following the murder of his six brother Jesuits in El Salvador.)

THINGS TO DO

▶ Read the text below which is from Luke's Gospel (1:46–55). Liberation theologians believe it contains the heart of their thinking. It is known as *The Magnificat*.

Mary said: My soul magnifies the Lord.
And my spirit rejoices in God my Saviour.
Because he has regarded the humility of his handmaid; for behold from henceforth all generations will call me blessed.
Because he that is mighty has done great things to me; and holy is his name.
And his mercy is from generation unto generation, to them that fear him.
He has shown might in his arm; he has scattered the proud in the conceit of their heart.
He has put down the mighty from their seat, and has exalted the humble.
He has filled the hungry with good things; and the rich he has sent empty away…
As he spoke to our fathers, to Abraham and to his seed for ever.

(Douay Version)

▶ Read carefully everything written in this unit and then say how you think Christians in developing countries would see themselves in this quote from Luke, attributed to Mary.

Bishop Clark, retiring bishop of East Anglia, in his cathedral grounds

The photo shows the Right Revd Alan Clark just before he retired as Bishop of the Diocese of East Anglia. He is sitting in the grounds of his Cathedral of St John the Baptist, in Norwich. This is a fairly new Catholic diocese, only formed in 1976 by a decree from Pope Paul VI, *Quod Ecumenicum*, for the counties of Cambridgeshire, Norfolk and Suffolk.

The Bishop is like a father to the people under his care, and most especially to the priests who assist him in his work. From time to time (as in the photograph on p. 95) they meet at the cathedral to celebrate Mass together and to express their unity with each other.

At the bishop's residence there are diocesan offices where the work of a busy organization goes on. The work is headed by priests appointed by the bishop and given the honorary title, Monsignor. There are many offices in the *Diocesan Curia*:

- The Chancery
- The Tribunal
- Finance Office
- Schools Commission
- Pastoral Council
- Council of Priests
- College of Consultors
- Department of Christian Formation (this includes a youth service, and commissions for adult and higher education, religious education, and vocational work).

- Liturgy Commission
- Ecumenism Commission
- Marriage and Family Life Commission
- Social Welfare Commission
- Justice and Peace Commission
- Communication Office (this includes press officers and representatives on TV and radio).

Many of the priests in the diocese have specialist responsibilities. Some work in ports, or in hospitals, in prisons or as school chaplains. There is usually a diocesan priest involved in pilgrimages, in work for the missions and in providing pastoral care for the deaf and hearing-impaired.

In every diocese there are dozens of Catholic organizations. These range from women's organizations, such as the Union of Catholic Mothers and the Catholic Women's Network, to medical groups, such as the Guild of Catholic Doctors and the Catholic Nurses Guild. There is an Association for Divorced and Separated Catholics, as well as a mutual support group for Catholic homosexuals, called *Quest*. There are groups that work for world peace (*Pax Christi*), and others that work to alleviate social problems (the Knights of St Columba and the St Vincent de Paul Society).

REFLECTION

A bishop should stand in the midst of his people as one who serves. Let him be a good shepherd who knows his sheep and whose sheep know him. Let him be a true father who excels in the spirit of love and solicitude for all...Let him so gather and mould the whole family of his flock that everyone, conscious of his own duties, may live and work in the communion of love.

(Vatican II Decree on Bishops 16)

Catholic priests gather for a diocesan celebration

The cathedral altar-servers prepare for a celebration Mass

A ROMAN CATHOLIC PARISH

St George's Church is one of the parishes in the diocese of East Anglia.

Father Philip, as seen by a young parishioner

Father Philip Shryane, the parish priest, has an assistant priest and two permanent deacons. Parishes work alongside the Catholic schools in the area. Christopher drew this portrait of Fr Philip after he had visited Christopher's class at school!

There are four hospitals and a prison to visit within the parish boundaries, so the priests have a group of nuns who help with the parish work. The laity organize most of the parish activities, from music for the liturgy and pre-school play groups to youth groups and the Society of St Vincent de Paul.

The photo top right shows some of the boys leading a procession celebrating a parish feast. You will notice that all the people in the photos in this unit are male. Girls in the parish are pleased that the Pope has at last given his approval to girl altar-servers.

THINGS TO DO

▶ Find out about the Roman Catholic diocese in which you live.

▶ Visit a Catholic church near you. Draw a rough sketch of the interior. In groups of four compare your pictures. Make a list of common features.

▶ Invite a parish priest to one of your lessons. Prepare questions to ask him.

▶ Invite a priest from the diocesan office to visit your class. Ask him to describe the work of the Commissions and other diocesan organizations.

◇

One group that works in every Roman Catholic diocese is the Society of St Vincent de Paul (SVP). In 1830 seven students living in war-torn Paris felt they should do something to help their neighbours. They wanted to show the same concern for others that Jesus showed in the Gospels. The local nuns gave them names of people in need of some help: the hungry, wounded or lonely. Within a few years, so many young people joined the original seven students that they decided to divide into groups called 'conferences', and to agree to a few regulations. They chose St Vincent de Paul for their patron because 200 years earlier he had shown a similar concern for the poor.

In 1844 the first SVP conference was started in London and spread rapidly around the country. Today, the groups, including both older and younger members of a parish, are spread around the world – in 116 countries.

The SVP is a voluntary organization, working from parishes, and offering all kinds of service to the homeless, families in distress, prisoners and their families, people living in poverty at home and abroad, the lonely and the sick.

Many Catholic schools have set up their own SVP conference run by the students themselves and united with each other through their Youth Office. They have their own newsletter, the *Young Vincentian*.

Children's summer camps

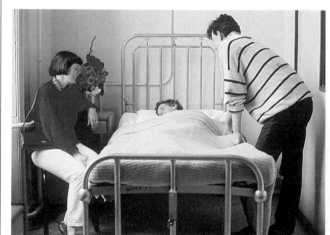

Hospital visiting

Community Care

Furniture stores providing for those in need

A St Vincent de Paul sister (Daughter of Charity) in Sierra Leone

THINGS TO DO

Answer the questions about organization in the Roman Catholic Church.

▶ Describe the traditional organization of the Catholic Church (i.e. triangular).

▶ Describe the newer organization of the Catholic Church (i.e. circular).

▶ Which of these two structures do you think works best? Give reasons for your answer.

▶ What is meant by liberation theology?

▶ Rigoberta Menchu of Guatemala won the Nobel Peace Prize in 1992 for her human rights' activities. She said:

'I am one who walks on the earth, not one who believes that the Kingdom of God comes only after death. Through all that I experienced, through so much pain and suffering, I learned what the role of a committed Christian is, above all, to condemn and denounce injustices against the people.'

In what way is Rigoberta a product of liberation theology?

▶ Draw a chart that could be placed in the Catholic diocesan offices to show how the diocese is organized.

My role as a priest

The role of the priest is changing by the day. The present administrative structures don't allow the priest to work in partnership with a living Church community. There are three or four different congregations that meet for Mass on a Sunday, but some of these people never meet each other. The priest can't get to know them.

However, the Church of God is not limited to its priests. Thank God the Holy Spirit is blowing through the Church and reminding all of us that we each have a part to play. One of the most exciting developments in recent times is that the laity are being allowed to be sharers in the mission of the Church.

For us priests, this is wonderful news. We can be freed to do the things we were ordained for. The laity can do the things that they are much more qualified to deal with than we are. Yes, it means that the priest relinquishes his power role and becomes more of a servant, and an animator of, and to, the parish family to which he belongs.

Let us pray for the courage to work towards the new horizons to which the Holy Spirit is calling us.

(Monsignor John Drury)

THINGS TO DO

▶ Monsignor Drury spent several years in South America. Do you think his ideas for parishes in Britain have been influenced by his work in Peru? Give reasons for your answer.

▶ In what ways can the laity take on the responsibilities of the parish?

KEY WORDS

Ethics and **morality** – both the Greek *ethos* and the Latin *mores* mean 'what is characteristic and customary'. In the actual use of the words, **ethics** has come to mean the characteristic way one behaves to fit into an orderly society. **Morality** refers to the objective rightness of the actions people perform. The distinction between the two is thin.

From the moment we are born we begin to learn how to behave in society. This is called 'socialization'; and we learn in many different ways.

What influences has Blanca (pictured below) already had in forming her understanding of good behaviour? Indeed, what do we mean by 'good'? She has been influenced by:

- her immediate family
- her relations
- her school friends
- her teachers
- the clubs she has joined
- the books she has read
- the television she watches
- the music she listens to
- the Church she attends.

Blanca

How does she actually know what is good behaviour? How does she know what is right and what is wrong? The answer is not straightforward. Here are some of the difficult questions she will discuss with her friends or family, or read about in the newspapers and magazines:

- Is it *always* wrong to steal? What if you are starving?
- Is a doctor who performs an abortion a murderer?
- Was the Christian, Bonhoeffer, right to have plotted to kill Hitler?
- Is it wrong to have sex before marriage?

Not everyone will give the same answer to these questions. Some people will express their own opinions with great passion, and yet be unable to give any reasons for their point of view. Yet, in the end, each of us has to make moral judgements for ourselves. Christians, however, believe that good guidance is available for this difficult task.

THE LANGUAGE OF ETHICS

In order to understand the Roman Catholic Church's position on morality, it is necessary to understand the basic ideas and language of ethics used by moralists in general. Here are some examples:

- In making an ethical judgement conscience is always involved (see p. 86).
- Goodness, according to the philosopher Aristotle, is something which fulfils its purpose. This idea was developed by St Thomas Aquinas in the Natural Law theory. This is very important in Roman Catholic moral teaching. Right action is what fulfils a natural purpose. Whatever frustrates a natural purpose is wrong.
- Goodness comes from God and is revealed by him. Good actions are those that conform to God's will.
- Moral judgements (about rightness and wrongness) fall into two categories, teleological and deontological.

Teleological judgements are based entirely on the end results of an action (*telos* is a Greek word meaning 'end').

Deontological judgements are based on a set of rules which must be obeyed (*deon* is a Greek word meaning 'must'). Acts are right or wrong in themselves, not because of the end result.

FOR DISCUSSION

Which of the following are teleological and which are deontological judgements?

1 'I have to tell the truth even though it will mean getting you into trouble, not me.'
2 'I must tell a lie in order to save her life.'
3 'A baby now would ruin her career, so she will have to have an abortion.'
4 'His suffering is terrible, but euthanasia is murder.'

HOW ROMAN CATHOLICS MAKE MORAL DECISIONS

The ultimate authority for Christians is God. His will has been made known (revealed) in:

- the Bible
- the life and teaching of Jesus
- the teaching of the Church
- the inspiration of the Holy Spirit
- actions undertaken in love
- one's conscience.

Christian moral behaviour depends on the relative authority given to these, and to the way they are interpreted. On many issues the Churches speak with a common voice. But there are areas of disagreement because Churches and individuals interpret 'authority' in different ways. Some Christians emphasize clear, absolute rules of behaviour and the only problem is in applying them. Others emphasize the responsibility of individuals or groups reaching their own decisions. Their difficulty is in the process of discerning God's will.

The Roman Catholic Church emphasizes loyalty to the authoritative moral code developed over the years, based on Scripture, Church tradition, and the official *Magisterium* (see p. 83). This has recently been re-emphasized by the Pope in an encyclical letter, *Veritatis Splendor* (*The Splendour of Truth*). In it he tells Catholics to be wary of moral decisions based on teleological grounds. The end does not justify the means. He also reinforces the Catholic Church's official disapproval of two moral systems used by many people today:

1 Utilitarianism

The system was developed by British-born Jeremy Bentham and John Stuart Mill in the eighteenth century. They claimed that 'the greatest good of the greatest number' is the best rule to take when making moral decisions.

2 Situation ethics

Thirty years ago the Anglican theologian Joseph Fletcher wrote that moral decisions should be based not on rules but on the general principal of love. He claimed that no rule can be absolute, and that each situation had to be judged for itself, on the basis of love (in the biblical sense of **Agape**).

'BE YE PERFECT'

The Catholic Church's moral teaching on most issues sets extremely high standards, like the Gospel. But the Church is also aware that people do not easily rise to such perfect ideals and so has developed a system of strong *pastoral* care for members. The Church, like St Paul, aims to help people discover God's love and power in their weakness.

THINGS TO DO

▶ Write your own definitions for the following:

1 A teleological judgement
2 A deontological judgement
3 Goodness according to Aristotle
4 Utilitarianism
5 Situation ethics

▶ Describe two different ways Christians can make moral decisions.

▶ Look at page 98 for a list of influences that have helped the girl in the photo to make moral choices. Consider each one in turn. Then make your own personal profile recognizing the different ways you have been influenced.

In this unit and Units 50–58 topics are looked at only from the Roman Catholic viewpoint. You will need to consult other books and sources of information for further ideas about the issues.

Should I give in to his charms?

There's a boy at college who seems so gentle and kind. He never bullies the young kids and everyone likes him. But he never goes out with a girl unless it's a dead cert that she'll sleep with him.

He's shown interest in me lately and I know he's going to ask me out. My friends say that, at 17, it's about time I 'did it' anyway. They think that if I like him as much as I say, I'd be stupid not to. But I'm scared of getting Aids. All the same, I don't know if I'm strong enough to say no. He's so gorgeous.

■ I understand your desires, but please don't let your heart rule your head. By refusing to sleep with someone with such a colourful sexual history, you're not only eluding Aids, you're also avoiding pregnancy and the chance of contracting other sexually transmitted diseases.

Publicity about Aids has pushed sexually transmitted diseases out of the spotlight but genital warts (which increase the risk of cervical cancer), gonorrhoea and herpes are still with us.

If you're determined to give romance a try with him, at least make it clear that you've no intention of making love until you're ready to. If the day comes when you do feel ready, insist he has a test at a special clinic first and uses condoms.

But think hard – maybe you'd rather wait until you meet someone who knows what a loving relationship is all about, before you commit yourself.

(Take a Break, August 1994)

You have probably read dozens of letters similar to the one above in magazines. Notice several things: that the girl is being pressurized by her friends to have sexual intercourse with a comparative stranger; that it is only the threat of Aids that deters her; that the agony aunt suggests she might wait until she knows what a loving relationship is.

Today, many young people are given the impression that relationships begin with sexual intercourse. It is not only Christians who teach that this is false; many people are convinced that the purpose of sex is not to initiate a loving relationship, but to complete it and make it permanent. Many young people later admit that they regret having had sex too early. Even so, it is estimated that by the year 2000, four out of every five couples marrying in England and Wales will have cohabited (lived together) first. Nowadays it is, therefore, generally assumed that a loving relationship includes sexual activity before marriage.

The Catholic Church teaches otherwise, though its teaching on marriage has had a chequered history. Jesus himself had little to say about human relationships and sexual activity, so the first teaching was taken from Greek philosophers like Aristotle. They presumed that the male carried the entire foetus in his semen, and that the woman was a mere 'incubator'. Such early distortion was bound to have unfortunate consequences. Clement of Alexandria, for example, a third-century theologian, concluded from Aristotle that 'to have a sexual relationship for any purpose other than to produce children is to violate nature'. This idea has dominated Catholic teaching ever since.

In the fifth century St Augustine taught that marriage should be indissoluble, quoting Mark's Gospel (10:6–10) and the suggestion in Ephesians 5:22–3 that it is a sign of the union between Christ and the Church. It was not until the thirteenth century that marriage was described as a sacrament by St Thomas Aquinas; and not until the Council of Trent, three centuries later, that the strict concept of the indissolubility of a marriage partnership was made into a law, and not merely an ideal.

Sexual ethics have changed rapidly in Europe and it leaves the Catholic Church looking, in many people's eyes, rather old fashioned. Older parents share the anxieties of many Church leaders that something very important is being lost. The papal document *Veritatis Splendor* remains rather rigid in its attitude towards marriage, and so too does the Catechism of the Catholic Church. Yet Catholic psychiatrist Jack Dominian points out that the changes taking place today do not necessarily mean a loss of integrity on the part of the young, only a shift in understanding what the sexual act itself is about. For centuries, Catholics thought that sexual intercourse was solely for creating babies. It is only in recent years that sexual pleasure has been recognized by the Church as being of equal importance, and welcomed as a gift from God for the mutual support of the partners.

HOMOSEXUALITY

The Catechism remains strongly 'traditional' on this subject, too, and restates the Church's view on homosexual relationships: 'Homosexual persons are called to chastity'. However, the harsh tone of the past ('homosexual acts are intrinsically disordered') has been softened. The Catholic Church condemns any prejudice shown against the homosexual community, while maintaining that actively sexual partnerships cannot be approved.

Roman Catholic teaching maintains that human love is a precious gift, a sharing in the life and love of God himself. Unselfish love between persons is itself a way to God. It enriches the human personality. In married love a couple come together in a life-long, life-giving union in which they give themselves totally and exclusively to each other. To be fully human and self-giving that love has to remain open to the possibility of new life. It provides the stability and affection necessary for the nurturing and development of the growing child. For all these reasons, the full sexual expression of love is reserved for husband and wife within marriage.

The Roman Catholic Church, therefore, cannot be expected to lend support to any measures which tacitly accept, even if they do not encourage, sexual activity outside marriage. To do so would be inconsistent. It would weaken our primary witness to the Christian vision of human love and marriage. Nor do we accept that for the unmarried the choice lies solely between condoms and infection. There is a third course of action: refusal to engage in extramarital sexual activity. Such self-discipline is not emotionally destructive, but can be a positive affirmation of a radical ideal, demanding but not impossible.

The Roman Catholic Church is committed to the cause of marriage and family life. It is a sad reflection on present values that no political party offers a coherent and comprehensive policy to sustain and uphold family life. Here there is much common ground to be explored. It is essential to enhance the quality of individual and family life.

A radical change in popular attitudes is possible, indeed necessary. Many in recent years have become convinced of the need to embrace a simpler, healthier life-style in order to enjoy a fuller, longer life. We are already changing deep-rooted habits in eating, drinking, smoking, exercise. How much greater is the necessity to rediscover the joy of faithful love and lasting marriage. It calls for self-discipline, restraint and a new awareness. Such a profound change in society also needs a comprehensive campaign of public education and persuasion.

(From an article by Cardinal Hume
in *The Times*, 7 January 1987)

The girl in the letter at the start of this unit was worried about Aids. Her friends would simply tell her that a condom was the answer. In the above extract from *The Times*, Cardinal Hume outlines the Church's moral teaching on sexuality.

PASTORAL CONCERN

'I am sad at the number of young women and girls who come to me for help. They have been pressured into sexual activity without any accompanying love and tenderness. They feel used and betrayed. My role is never to condemn, only to pick up the hurt women, to reassure them that God loves and treasures them; that they are still beautiful in his sight. They need their dignity restored. I am glad that as a priest, I seem able to do this.'

(Fr John, RC parish priest)

Men and women do not choose their homosexual condition…They must be accepted with respect, compassion and sensitivity. Every sign of unjust discrimination in their regard should be avoided.

(*Catechism of the Catholic Church*, No. 2358)

REFLECTION

'Should the Church move with the times?' The answer must be 'Yes'. Society has a lot to teach the Church about sex. But Christianity too embodies fundamental truths which – although in need of equally fundamental rethinking themselves – carry basic values which society ignores at its peril.

(Jack Dominian)

THINGS TO DO

▶ Jack Dominian writes of 'basic values which society ignores at its peril'. What are these basic values? Why do you suppose he thinks that society ignores them at its peril?

▶ 'Until death us do part.' Comment on this statement taken from the marriage service. Explain its importance to Roman Catholics.

Marriage is like twirling a baton, turning handsprings, or eating with chopsticks; it looks so easy till you try it.

(Helen Rowland)

All marriages are happy. It's living together afterwards that causes all the trouble.

(Farmer's Almanac)

A successful marriage is an edifice that must be rebuilt every day.

(André Maurois)

We bandy about the word love without realizing how much effort is required in sustaining it.

(Jack Dominian)

These are the sort of wise sayings that might be heard at a wedding reception – a warning to the newly wed couple that marriage is hard work and the future will not necessarily always run smoothly. The priest at the marriage ceremony will already have outlined the high ideals set for a Christian, by reminding them of the Gospel call for a lifelong union:

In the beginning, at the time of creation, God made the male and female. And for this reason a man will leave his father and mother and unite with his wife, and the two will become one. So they are no longer two, but one. Man must not separate, then, what God has joined together.

(Jesus according to *Mark 10:6–9*)

When two people live together, and especially when children arrive, there are bound to be difficulties and conflict. Sometimes external pressures can become intolerable and put the relationship under severe strain. Some people can survive stress, but others cope less well, for various reasons. With early support from family and friends, or professional help from RELATE or the Catholic Marriage Advisory Council, some couples survive the crisis. But it is a distressing fact that Britain has the highest rate of divorce in Europe. Catholic families are part of these statistics.

THE CATHOLIC CHURCH AND DIVORCE

In the Catholic Church a validly contracted marriage between two baptized Christians is regarded as a sacrament. If this marriage is consummated (the couple have sexual intercourse), then it cannot be dissolved. The Church bases this strict law on the words of Jesus in Mark's Gospel. It can be argued that Jesus did not say very much about marriage, but as one person has commented:

He didn't need to. His teaching was all about priorities, relationships, the value we place on the other person, our answerability to one another, and to God.

(Wendy Green)

However, the Church can dissolve and annul a marriage. There is a distinction.

1 Dissolving a marriage

a   For a serious reason, perfectly valid marriages can be dissolved if neither or only one of the partners is baptized. In the former case, if one partner wishes to be baptized and become a Christian, and the other partner refuses to live peacefully from then on, they may separate under what is known as the 'Pauline Privilege'. St Paul wrote: 'If the unbelieving partner desires to separate, let it be so; in such a case the baptized partner is not bound. For "God has called us to peace." ' (1 Corinthians 7:15) If there is a breakdown of marriage in which only one of the persons is baptized, then what is known as the 'Petrine Privilege' allows the baptized partner to leave in order to marry another baptized person. Even the unbaptized partner may leave to marry a baptized person, provided they themselves become baptized.

b   A second ground for dissolving a marriage, even one which would normally be regarded as a sacrament, is when it has not been consummated. This could be because of impotence or the inability to assume the obligations of marriage.

2 Marriage annulment

If a marriage is thought to be null or invalid, i.e. never a real marriage at all, the partners can petition the diocesan Tribunal. The Tribunal will take evidence from the couple and witnesses, and prepare a case to go before the 'Defender of the Bond' (of marriage). The Defender presents the case to three judges, and their decision then goes on appeal to three more judges. All these judges are qualified in the Canon Law of the Church. The decisions are made locally, not in Rome.

The grounds for declaring a marriage null are:

- A lack of consent, e.g. one partner was forced into the marriage

- A lack of judgement, e.g. when one or both partners marry without being fully aware of what marriage is about

- A lack of intention, i.e. if either partner at the time of marriage denies any one of the three elements of a Catholic marriage, which is for life, with one partner, and remains open to bearing children.

- Inability to take on the duties of marriage, e.g. through psychological or mental illness.

SEPARATION AND CIVIL DIVORCE

Catholic couples who find it impossible to continue living together, and who have no grounds for dissolving or annulling the marriage, can apply to the Church for an official separation, and even confirm this separation in a civil divorce according to the 1969 Divorce Act. They are free to do this, though Church authorities are worried that the Act has devalued marriage and made divorce easy. Divorced Catholics are expected to remain single and not enter into a second marriage. The Church cannot officially bless a second union.

There are many people who admire the Catholic Church's strict teaching on marriage. But there are also those, including bishops and priests, who find the severity of the rules difficult to reconcile with pastoral care. Many Catholics are worried that, in spite of the Pope's words (in the Pastoral Concern box on this page), divorce is seen as a stigma, and divorced and remarried Catholics are kept on the edges of the Church.

THE CATHOLIC MARRIAGE ADVISORY COUNCIL

The Catholic Marriage Advisory Council (CMAC) is a professional organization that offers help to distressed couples or individuals.

Sometimes people feel imprisoned within their marriage, trapped perhaps, not wanting to leave, yet longing for that freedom to love freely. This may imply that our partners hold us prisoner but it may be our memories which hold us fast. It is possible to begin to break the pattern of hurt, rejection and fear. To be helped to understand ourselves, to forgive ourselves, to love ourselves and to believe that we can be lovable and loving, releasing us from the prison of despair. We can only love others to the extent that we love ourselves and if that love is limited we are impoverished. To share the fear and confusion of our lives with a professionally trained counsellor can be enlightening and liberating.

(CMAC)

CMAC has counsellors in 84 centres in the UK, available to anyone regardless of marital status or belief.

PASTORAL CONCERN

We must reach out with love – the love of Christ – to those who know the pain of failure in marriage; to those who know the loneliness of bringing up a family on their own; to those whose family life is dominated by tragedy or by illness of mind or body.

(Pope John Paul II, 31 May 1982 in York)

THINGS TO DO

▶ What do you think are the main reasons for today's marriage breakdowns?

▶ Write a short fictional story about a young married person who could fit the description in the CMAC advertisement.

▶ On what grounds is the Catholic Church so strict about divorce?

'I remember saying to my daughter, "If you're going to have sex, just be sure you take precautions". But the truth is that I don't want my daughter having casual sex, and what I was saying wasn't helping her to understand my values or how I felt.'

'I told him I had my first baby before I married his father. I didn't justify it. At least it wasn't casual sex, I said, but I was sorry it had happened like that, and I wouldn't like him to make the same mistake.'

'She wouldn't sleep with her boyfriend, and he broke off with her. She was very upset. So I gave her I Married You by Walter Trobisch. She read it on the train that night, and when she came home she said: "Thanks a lot for that book. It helped me to see that he wasn't right for me." '

These three parents were discussing the ways they talked to their children about sexual relationships. Parents can find this very difficult. Both parents and teachers can be confused into thinking that most young people will be having sexual intercourse as soon as they have a girl/boy friend. It is the easy access to contraceptives that makes this a possibility. Today, adults can feel that they are swimming against the current; against the influence of the media, against teenage culture and against the pressure of peer groups.

Contraception refers to the various methods by which a couple can avoid a pregnancy. All Christian denominations disapprove of young people using contraceptives outside of marriage. But it is only the Catholic Church that puts a total ban on their use. The Church believes that intercourse is sinful even in a married relationship if the procreation of children is hindered in an artificial way. In his 1968 encyclical, *Humanae Vitae*, Pope Paul VI confirmed earlier teaching that all artificial forms of contraception are forbidden, including the condom. In the light of the AIDS situation, many people find this difficult to understand.

The Catholic Church teaching appeals to a morality based on the Natural Law. This was developed by St Thomas Aquinas in the thirteenth century, following the teaching of the philosopher Aristotle, and presumes that the right thing to do is that which is in accordance with nature itself. Artificial contraceptives always interfere with the natural act of intercourse, so they are always wrong. Not all Christians accept that the 'Natural Law' is so absolute.

FAMILY PLANNING

Many people imagine that the Church encourages Catholic parents to have very large families. This is no longer true. The Catechism leaves the choice to parents:

> *A particular aspect of responsibility (in marriage) concerns the regulation of births. For just reasons, spouses may wish to space the births of their children. It is their duty to make certain that their desire is not motivated by selfishness but is in conformity with the generosity appropriate to responsible parenthood.*
>
> (*Catechism of the Catholic Church*, No. 2368)

The four natural ways of birth control, acceptable to Catholics are:

1 Withdrawal

The man withdraws his penis from the woman's vagina before his sperm is released. This is not considered a safe way as sperm can be released at any time.

2 Rhythm

The couple have sex only during the days in the woman's menstrual cycle when it is regarded 'safe' because she is not fertile. This is worked out by taking her temperature regularly. For this method to be successful the woman needs to have an extremely regular cycle.

3 NFP (Natural Family Planning)

A woman can observe the natural signs and symptoms of fertility in her body, and by recording them she can plan or prevent a pregnancy. There is the temperature method, the Billings ovulation method, and a combination of both called the Sympto-thermal method. As this is regarded as one of the safest methods of birth control, it is favoured by many Catholic couples.

4 Abstinence

For those who find the above methods difficult or even unworkable, abstinence from sexual intercourse is the only way of preventing conception.

YOUNG PEOPLE AND CONTRACEPTION

US teenagers get their kicks from chastity

There is a new buzzword beginning to travel the classrooms and recreation yards of America and it has nothing to do with records or airliners. It is 'virgin', as in 'I'm gonna stay a...'. The movement is still small, but its momentum is evidently growing.

'Virgin clubs' are being formed in schools around the country and purity before marriage has become the topic of magazine and television features. Twenty five years after Woodstock, it is the new counter-culture.

Its strength was on display in Washington two weekends ago when followers of 'True Love Waits', a church-based campaign dedicated to promoting sexual abstinence, descended on the Mall in front of Congress and staked into the turf more than 200,000 white pledge-cards, each one signed by a young person swearing off intercourse until marriage. The few words on the cards are bland enough, but radical. 'Believing that true love waits, I make a commitment to God, myself, my family, those I date, my future mate, and my future children to be sexually pure until the day I enter a covenant marriage relationship.'

(*The Independent*, 11 August 1994)

The availability of contraceptives has certainly encouraged early sexual experience. Films, soap operas, videos, and teenage magazines seem to presume that all young people have sex and will 'take precautions' to prevent pregnancy and AIDS. The newspaper article about US teenagers suggests that some young people are not going to be pressured into accepting this situation.

New school materials are coming onto the market in Britain which also uphold the value of virginity and celibacy. Notes accompanying a video for schools, *Make Love Last*, include texts such as this:

Christians would agree that the option for abstinence from sexual relations outside of marriage, even celibacy, is a way of life which Christ modelled and it is therefore to be valued. ... Sex education which only focuses on safer-sex or which assumes the acceptability of multiple partners and sexual experimentation during adolescence, is unacceptable to most Christians who wish their children to grow up to honour marriage and to see the positive benefits of seeking sexual fulfilment with one life-long partner.

(*Make Love Last*, Teachers' Pack)

The video itself is presented by young people who make a strong case for sexual abstinence.

THINGS TO DO

▶ On what grounds does the Catholic Church ban artificial contraception?

▶ Outline the four methods of birth control open to Catholics.

▶ In groups of four, discuss the following statements:

● 'Society has become immoral because of the easy access to contraception.'

● 'The Catholic Church is old fashioned in its view on contraception. No one takes its teaching seriously.'

● 'The example of the US teenagers is just what we need. Sexual abstinence is what many young people really want.'

'With the full force of British law, we sanction every day the destruction of 600 unborn children, a total of nearly four million since the passage of the 1967 legislation. We sanction destructive experiments on the human embryo, we sanction the killing of the unborn baby even during birth if it has a minor form of handicap or disability. It shows how far secularism and utilitarianism have won the day. Even if as a Christian I was in a minority of one, that wouldn't allow me to remain silent on this issue. But you don't have to be Christian to be pro-life. What brings me great encouragement is that people from other faiths, including Islam and Buddhism, and some with no faith, are increasingly coming to see that, from the destruction of human life, stem many of the other degradations we see today in our society.'

(David Alton MP)

Many people argue that statements and statistics such as the one above are emotive and should not be given publicity as they blur the issue of abortion. Christians are likely to disagree because they have such strong views about the sanctity of life. Catholics regard the killing of an unborn child as morally wrong. Their teaching is based upon a belief that life begins at the moment of conception, and that a foetus has the same right to life as its mother. This applies even to a foetus likely to develop as a handicapped baby. To abort such a foetus, would, for a Catholic, be a serious denial of the dignity of each human person.

There are Christians who do not take such a strict line, and who would use a utilitarian or situation ethics argument (see p. 99) to defend cases where an abortion could be allowed; e.g. where the mother's life is in danger, where someone has been raped, or where the foetus is seriously deformed.

The abortion issue arouses deep emotion. There is a danger that people with religious beliefs may disregard the seriousness and integrity of those who take a pro-abortion view. In the same way, those who support abortion as 'a woman's right to choose' can easily dismiss all anti-abortionists as sentimental or religious cranks.

FOR DISCUSSION

Discuss the following arguments taken from opposing sides. Try to argue in favour of a position that you would not naturally take. Work in groups of four.

- 'The unborn child has the same rights as you and me.'

- 'A foetus is only a potential human life, so it cannot have the same rights as its mother.'

- 'To abort a damaged foetus is to tell all disabled people their lives are not worth much.'

- 'Abortion saves thousands of children from unwanted, miserable lives.'

REFLECTIONS

From the time the ovum is fertilized, a life is begun which is neither that of the father nor the mother. It is the life of a new human being with its own growth. It would never become human if it were not human already.

(Roman Catholic Declaration on Procured Abortion, 1974)

God has created us to love and to be loved, in his own image, as evidence of his love. For this reason I say that abortion is the greatest evil. If any one of you does not want his own child, do not kill it, but give it to me.

(Mother Teresa)

PASTORAL CONCERN

Official Church teaching is uncompromising over abortion. But there are organizations, such as the LIFE movement and SPUC (Society for the Protection of the Unborn Child), that offer counselling, support and material help to women or girls who are pregnant and in distress.

POPULATION CONTROL AND ABORTION

The Vatican accused the United Nations Population Fund of promoting abortion on demand in their annual report. 'The future of humanity is under discussion,' said a papal official. He is wrong about the UN report. It is markedly unenthusiastic about abortion, quoting World Bank estimates that it accounts for at least 60,000 maternal deaths a year. The report specifically calls for better family planning information and services to minimize recourse to abortion.

Of course the Catholic Church is also against family planning. In a strange move the Church has united with fundamentalist Muslims in opposing the United Nations. These Muslims depict birth-control and abortion as a Western conspiracy to keep down the world population of Muslims and corrupt Muslim women.

There is a real population problem. It stands now at 5.66 billion. Assuming continued declining fertility it could be 10 billion in 2050. Without it, the figure could be 12.2 billion. Global agriculture could be expanded to feed that number. But the productive areas are in the wrong place and are produced at the wrong price. More serious is the lack of water.

The doctrine that poverty is the main cause of high birth rates – poor families need large families to earn for them – has been largely superseded. Experience shows that when poor women are given a choice they opt for fewer children. The main message from the UN is the need to empower women, to give them choice. That is what Muslim fundamentalists want least. It is sad that the Vatican should join them.

(Adapted from an article in *The Independent*, 11 August 1994)

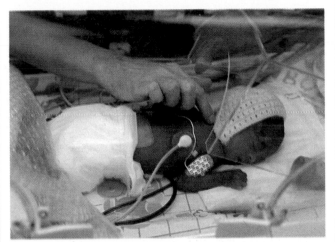
Special medical care to help a premature baby born at 24 weeks

THINGS TO DO

▶ Answer the following questions on the article from *The Independent*:

1 Why has the Vatican opposed the United Nations Population Fund?
2 Why does the reporter believe the papal official was wrong about the UN report?
3 Why have Muslim fundamentalists joined the argument?
4 The Church has always taught that the problem is not overpopulation but economic distribution of food. What has the article to say about this?
5 'The article is really about women's rights.' Would you agree? Explain your answer.
6 Imagine you are a Catholic representative at the population conference. How would you defend the Church's position on family planning and abortion in view of the massive increase in population that is predicted?

Footnote
In the event the Vatican registered its reservations about the UN proposals for population control at the Cairo conference in September 1994. But the Vatican spokesman, recognizing the real problem of population growth, did not vote against the proposals.

I will use treatment to help the sick according to my ability and judgement, but never with a view to injury and wrongdoing. Neither will I administer a poison to anybody when asked to do so, nor will I suggest such a course. Similarly I will not give to a woman a pessary to cause abortion. But I will keep pure and holy both my life and art.

(Part of the Hippocratic Oath)

Hippocrates, who lived in the fourth century BC, is known as the founder of modern medicine. He wrote an oath for doctors based on a principal *primum non nocere* – 'first do no harm'. This established the trust a patient should always have in a doctor. This trust survived centuries, but was shaken in Nazi Germany when doctors experimented on people in the concentration camps. When these war crimes were examined, the British Medical Association (BMA) stated:

Research in medicine as well as its practice must never be separated from eternal moral values.

(*War Crimes and Medicine*, 1947)

The same document endorsed a recommendation from the World Medical Association to draft a modern version of the Hippocratic Oath which still binds all doctors, and is part of their graduation ceremony. This was done in 1948, in the 'Declaration of Geneva'. It states:

The health of my patient will be my first consideration…I will have the utmost respect for human life from the moment of conception.

Also in 1948, the National Health Service was established in Britain. For Catholics this meant the state was doing everything their faith encouraged – free care for the sick whatever their background.

Today, there is anxiety amongst many people, including Christians, that this established moral framework is being eroded, especially by the renewed discussion about euthanasia.

WHAT IS EUTHANASIA?

The Catholic Church issued a *Declaration on Euthanasia* in 1980 and defined euthanasia as 'an action or omission which, either of itself or by intention, causes death'.

The Church's position on euthanasia

● A doctor gives drugs to a patient with the main purpose of relieving pain, but as a 'side effect' the patient has an earlier death. This is not euthanasia as the intention was to relieve pain.

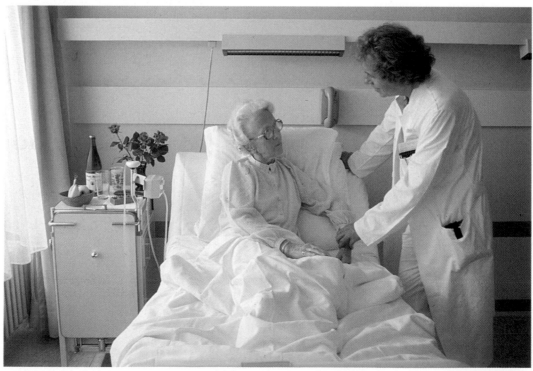

The relationship of trust between a doctor and an elderly patient would be threatened if euthanasia were law

- A doctor is asked for drugs, the sole purpose of which is to bring death. This is euthanasia and is condemned by the Church and the BMA.

- A patient is dying and there is no chance of survival, but temporary resuscitation is possible with new technology. It requires extraordinary means to do this and the Church recognizes that it is inappropriate. This is not euthanasia.

The Catechism of the Catholic Church restated its position, arguing against euthanasia as follows:

1 Only God has the right to take life. Suffering has its own value. The moment of death is too important to take out of God's hands.
2 Legal euthanasia would put pressure on the elderly or sick to take the 'burden' off their family.
3 Legal euthanasia would make it all too easy for doctors to 'save money' by getting rid of elderly patients.
4 The hospice movement has removed the need even to think about euthanasia. People, through palliative (painkilling) care, can die in dignity, free from pain.
5 Euthanasia can become the 'thin end of the wedge'. Once the principle is accepted, the consequence may be horrific; e.g. 'We can get rid of people with disabilities.'

The recent case of Tony Bland has brought euthanasia back into the headlines. In 1989 hundreds of football fans were trampled in a stampede at the Hillsborough stadium in Sheffield. Sixteen-year-old Tony was one of them. He never regained consciousness, but was kept alive on a life-support machine for more than four years. Finally, his parents successfully brought a case before the Law Lords to stop feeding him and to turn off the machine. A Catholic priest, Fr James Morrow, tried to have the parents charged with murder, claiming to speak on behalf of the Catholic Church. A Catholic bishop disagreed with this action, and appealed to both sides to respect each other.

We need to consider what the cause is which can arouse such strong and contrary emotions. What links Fr Morrow's outrageous attempt to have the parents of Tony Bland indicted for murder and his invasion of private abortion clinics? It is the defence of human life…

The pro-lifers are right in coming to the defence of the defenceless, but they must not forget the other victims of circumstance. Nor should those who claim a right over their own bodies forget the rights of the unborn. Their bodies are no less sacrosanct.

(Bishop Mario Conti in *The Press and Journal*, 24 April 1993)

PASTORAL CONCERN

The decisions that face the medical profession are daunting. Doctors and nurses need support. Catholics have formed a Catholic Nurses Guild and a Guild of Catholic Doctors.

Considerable progress has recently been made in providing relief of pain, and care for the dying. Much of this work was initiated by Christians (see the hospice movement on p. 75).

Dr Robert George, who cares for people with AIDS at a hospice, says:

'…the only realistic way forward in providing a robust alternative to euthanasia is a widespread practice of high quality palliative medicine, and its incorporation into the standard undergraduate curriculum.'

THINGS TO DO

▶ It was suggested in the Dutch Parliament that newborn babies with severe malformation should be killed. Write a letter to the press opposing the suggestion.

▶ Read the Catechism's five arguments against euthanasia. How would a member of the Voluntary Euthanasia Society (a group which demands freedom of choice about euthanasia) answer these arguments?

In recent years, advances in medical science have made it possible for human fertilization to take place by artificial means. This has given joy to many couples, but has also presented a number of moral dilemmas. The Catholic Church, having based all its moral teaching on the Natural Law Theory, says that new life can only be created within the marriage union by natural means. It therefore disapproves of the seven techniques which have now become ordinary practice in medicine.

SEVEN FRONT-LINE TECHNIQUES IN HUMAN FERTILIZATION AND EMBRYOLOGY

1 *Artificial insemination by husband* (AIH). Putting male semen into a woman using an instrument.
2 *Artificial insemination by donor* (AID). The semen is provided by an anonymous donor and not the husband.
3 *In vitro fertilization* for husband and wife (IVF). (Test tube babies.) The ovum is withdrawn from the woman and fertilized with the man's semen under laboratory conditions. The embryo is then transferred to the womb.
4 *Egg donation.* A woman donates an ovum, which is then fertilized with the semen of the husband of the woman into whose uterus the resulting embryo is transferred.
5 *Embryo donation.* This is similar to egg donation, except the ovum is fertilized by semen from a donor because both partners are infertile or both carry a genetic defect.
6 *Surrogacy* ('womb-leasing'). A woman bears a child for another who cannot become pregnant, and hands over the child at birth.
7 *Scientific research on human embryos.* Potential research which ranges from simple study of early embryos in order to increase knowledge about the beginnings of human development (for infertility, etc.), to testing new drugs on embryos.

(Adapted from Joe Jenkins, *Contemporary Moral Issues*, 1992)

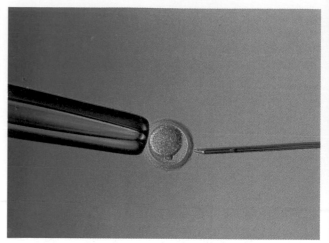

Microscope view of in vitro *fertilization. A human egg (ovum) is being injected with a sperm cell*

THE GOVERNMENT AND THE CHURCH

The government has always been cautious in the field of embryo research and is advised by a team which includes moral theologians. In 1982 a Committee of Inquiry into Human Fertilization and Embryology was set up and chaired by Dame Mary Warnock. The Catholic Church's 'Bishops' Joint Committee on Bio-Ethical Issues' sent a response to the Warnock Report, commenting on all 59 recommendations. On many issues there was agreement.

Parliament passed the Human Fertilization and Embryology Act in 1990. The Church is not wholly satisfied with the Act, although it applauds some of the guidelines. The *Catholic Truth Society* published a pamphlet outlining the Church's response. It covers four areas:

1 Human beings can never be treated as means to an end. The human embryo has human rights and therefore has to be treated with proper respect. ('Embryo' refers to the beginning of life from fertilization to eight weeks gestation. From then to birth (40 weeks) it is called a 'foetus'.
2 Society depends on stable family life. It is only in this loving background that sexual activity is appropriate.
3 Science must never take precedence over individual persons. This is especially so when they are defenceless.
4 Allocating resources to the health service of a nation is difficult. It is doubtful that the 'right' to have a child should take precedence over other areas of medicine.

THINGS TO DO

Prenatal diagnosis is morally licit if it respects the life and integrity of the embryo and the human foetus, and is directed toward its safeguarding or healing as an individual…It is gravely opposed to moral law when this is done with the thought of possibly inducing an abortion, depending upon the results: a diagnosis must not be the equivalent of a death sentence.

(*Catechism of the Catholic Church*, No. 2274)

▶ Rewrite the above quotation in your own words and then explain why you think the Church takes this view.

▶ There are four patients in hospital:

- Anne, 37, is waiting for the IVF programme.

- Tom, 55, is expecting his second hip operation.

- Sally, 69, needs a new kidney.

- Danny, 23, awaits delicate surgery on his knee (so that he can return to professional football).

Unfortunately, there is only enough money to perform one of the above operations. In groups of four, decide who shall have it. Role play the parts.

WHAT ABOUT ADOPTION?

The Pope suggests adoption would be the best answer for infertile couples. Unfortunately, it is not easy to adopt children, especially babies, in the UK. Many couples go abroad to find their families, but it is time consuming, expensive and often subject to chance, since both government and social services are unfavourably disposed towards overseas adoptions. With millions of abandoned babies in some countries and thousands of would-be parents in Europe, it has been suggested that there might perhaps be a role for the Catholic Church to set up a safe, honest network to arrange more of these adoptions.

Legacy of an adopted child

Once there were two women who never knew each other.
One you do not remember; the other you call mother.
Two different lives, shaped to make you one.
One became a guiding star; the other become your sun.
The first gave you life and the second taught you to live it.
The first gave you need for love and the second was there to give it.
One gave you a nationality, the other gave you a name.
One gave you the seed of talent, the other gave you an aim.
One gave you emotions, the other calmed your fears.
One saw your first sweet smile, the other dried your tears.
One gave you up…it was all that she could do.
The other prayed for a child and God led her straight to you.
And now you ask, through your fears
The age old questions, unanswered through the years.
Heredity or environment…which are you the product of…
Neither my darling…neither.
Just two different kinds of love.

(Author unknown)

FOR DISCUSSION

▶ In groups of four, discuss the possibility of a Catholic adoption network. Then prepare a letter giving your views either for the press, or for your local bishop.

Polluting the environment

Thou shalt not steal

(The seventh commandment)

Respect for the integrity of creation

The seventh commandment enjoins respect for the integrity of creation. Animals, like plants and inanimate beings, are by nature destined for the common good of past, present and future humanity. Use of the mineral, vegetable and animal resources of the universe cannot be divorced from respect for moral imperatives. Man's dominion over inanimate and other living beings granted by the Creator is not absolute; it is limited by the concern for the quality of life of his neighbour, including generations to come; it requires a religious respect for the integrity of creation.

Animals are God's creatures. He surrounds them with his providential care. By their mere existence they bless him and give him glory. Thus men owe them kindness. We should recall the gentleness with which saints like St Francis of Assisi or St Philip Neri treated animals.

(*Catechism of the Catholic Church*, No.s 2415, 2416)

This is the Catholic Church's official statement on environmental and animal issues. Until recently, the Genesis creation account ('They will have power over the fish, the birds and all the animals' – *Genesis 1:26*) was always taken by Christians as giving them a free hand to dominate and exploit the natural world, as if it was only there to serve their needs. It is only now, with the planet in crisis, that people have criticized this interpretation and suggested that Christians have been responsible for the neglect and abuse of the earth.

There are those who will say the Catechism does not do enough to disown this view, especially as a later text approves of some testing on animals 'when it remains in reasonable limits'.

There are, however, many Catholic voices in support of the numerous campaigns for the protection of the earth.

- CAFOD continually produces important education material.
- Bishops speak out in defence of individuals who work to save the planet (e.g. in praise of Chico Mendes who was killed as he spoke out to protect the Brazilian forests).
- Many parishes sell Traidcraft materials and advocate a better way to use the earth's resources.

In 1988, partly due to pollution suppressing their immune system, 15,000 seals died in a viral epidemic in the North Sea. This could happen again.

REFLECTIONS

Chico had a lot of faith in God, and the Church always supported him. People hid him in church when enemies were after him. God helps people. When Chico died I was filled with despair. But God comforted me and inspired me to work alongside others to carry on Chico's work. They killed him, but they didn't kill his ideas. We continue his battle.

(Wife of Chico Mendes)

In the last fifty years, the earth has been destroyed and devastated more than in all the millions of years behind us… If we want to live we have to do something immediately… Let us always have the eyes of St Francis to see God in everything. And the heart St Francis had, to call all that is alive, all that can be developed or restored, our sisters and brothers.

(Cardinal Arns of Brazil).

People read documents from a particular perspective. I came to read Veritatis Splendor, *the papal encyclical on the foundations of morality, with questions prompted by almost two decades of involvement with environmental issues…Given what is at stake, I was saddened that despite its length – 179 pages –* Veritatis Splendor *was silent on environmental issues…The encyclical deals with the universal and unchanging nature of moral norms and restates that particular moral acts like homicide, genocide, abortion and euthanasia are intrinsically evil. There is, however, no mention of the morality of biocide or geocide, the poisoning of the air, water and soil, nor the irreversible destruction of the rain forests. The morality of sexual, political and economic matters is discussed and clear norms enunciated. The perspective is exclusively God-centred and human-centred. It would appear that the drafters of the encyclical are blind to the moral implications of environmental destruction.*

(Sean McDonagh, 'Viewpoint', *The Tablet*, 30 April 1994)

THINGS TO DO

▶ Write 200 words on the pollution of the environment. Use the illustration on page 112 to help you.

▶ Create a class collage on this theme.

- One group should redraw the illustration on page 112 as large as possible.

- The rest of the class should draw hot-air balloons to represent groups or organizations that work to save the planet (agree on size before you start).

- Stick the hot-air balloons on the redrawn picture.

▶ Prepare a short assembly on environmental issues and use the collage as a backdrop.

▶ Write an essay on 'The Church and environmental issues.'

Those who watched television when black South Africans went to the polls for the first time, in April 1994, will never forget the sight of Archbishop Desmond Tutu casting his vote and then dancing for joy, singing 'Yipeee'. For him and all Christians, it was the moment they had always insisted had to come. They had used strikes, marches and speeches for decades, to remind politicians that all people, created in God's image, should be treated with dignity and equality in their country. When the apartheid system finally came to an end with the election of President Nelson Mandela, he thanked Christians for their part in bringing an end to the injustices.

It was taken for granted in South Africa that the Churches had a role in political activity. When Archbishop Tutu was warned not to mix religion with politics, he replied: 'Does it say anywhere that God is not interested in what happens from Monday to Saturday but only in what happens on Sunday?'

JESUS AND POLITICS

The political scene in Palestine at the time of Jesus was often violent. Most Jews deeply resented the Roman occupation, and terrorist movements grew up as people plotted to overthrow the foreign rule. One of the Apostles, Simon, had been a member of the Zealots, a revolutionary organization. Many of Jesus' followers expected him to lead them, as Messiah, to overthrow the Romans. But Jesus made it quite clear that this was not his way. He opted for a peaceful role and even forgave his enemies before he died.

From this, many Christians have argued that Jesus would take no part in politics; his message was entirely spiritual. They advocate that the Church should act in the same way. Not all Christians agree, as the South African experience shows. Many events in the Gospels demonstrate how Jesus challenged authority. He even argued against the law on occasions, and was always taking the side of the disadvantaged – those who had become victims of bad political policy.

WHERE DOES THE CATHOLIC CHURCH STAND?

Earlier in the book (Unit 45) we saw that more than one theology has developed in the Church as Catholics have applied the Gospel to their contemporary world. Two theologies in particular take a very different stand over politics and religion.

Archbishop Desmond Tutu casts his vote in the South African elections, April 1994

1 A two-world view

'The Church's role is a spiritual one. Leave politics to the politicians.'

(An MP)

This remark represents an older theology, based on a two-world view. There are two worlds, God's which is heaven, and humankind's which is 'down here' on earth. God is the transcendent father-creator, who can alter the rules if he wishes. People can get glimpses of God, especially in the life of Jesus who was sent down from heaven to save the world from sin. Jesus, the Son of God, points away from earth back to his real home in heaven. This earth is only temporary, a distraction from real life which is lived 'in God'. This theology led the early Christians to leave the world for monasteries, and it later influenced teaching which led the poor to believe that their lives on earth did not matter. True riches are in heaven, where those who had suffered down here would be rewarded.

'I chose you from this world, and you do not belong to it; that is why the world hates you.'

(John 15:19)

2 A global view

When God encounters injustice, oppression, exploitation, he takes sides. Then God and the Bible are subversive of such a situation.

(Archbishop Helder Camera)

This is a newer theology which approaches God from the opposite way. It has developed from the world we live in today – the global world. People know what is happening everywhere and feel responsible. Many Catholics today say they understand and meet God here, in this life, through human experience. They say that God is best understood in terms of love, and they see that most clearly in the human life of Jesus. His compassion and love was unique – we can therefore call him God's own Son. God, who created people in his image, is limited by his own creation. As long as there is poverty, injustice and greed God's plan is blocked. It is this call to free (liberate) the world that has been the cry of liberation theologians and Catholics who share their vision.

Whoever loves is a child of God and knows God. Whoever does not love does not know God. For God is love.

(1 John 4:7–8)

Catholics are not told that one theology is right and the other wrong. They learn to live within both traditions. Taking any one view to an extreme can distort the truth, and this is the anxiety of Church leaders. The difficulty lies in deciding what is extreme. Today Catholics who take the 'option for the poor' into politics (like the former priest, then President, Jean-Bertrand Aristide of Haiti, totally dedicated to his suffering people) have had little official support from the Church. But there have always been Catholic bishops who quietly confront politicians, and do encourage Catholics to enter political debate. Pope John Paul's recent encyclical letter, *Christifideles Laici* states that it is the fundamental duty of lay Christians to influence their society, not only in the home, but also in the workplace and in politics.

REFLECTIONS

Over the last hundred years the Church has developed very clear guidelines and encouragement for all Catholics to come out into the open in order to work to make the world a more just, compassionate and peaceful place.

We can do this by offering our time and talents in different ways. Union work, political campaigning, combating poverty in our own country, opposing racism in all its forms, protecting the rights of the unemployed and of minority groups, caring for the environment, controlling armaments dealing – these are just some examples of the Church 'party political'. Nor is it an optional extra for a few people in the parish. It is part of what it means to respond to the call of the Gospel today.

(Pastoral letter of Bishop Brewer, Lancaster, November 1991)

The poverty of the poor is not a summons to alleviate their plight with acts of generosity, but rather a compelling obligation to fashion an entirely different social order.

(Gustavo Gutierrez)

THINGS TO DO

▶ Write a dialogue between the MP quoted on p. 114 and Gustavo Gutierrez, discussing their opposing views on the relationship of the Church to politics.

▶ Read the newspaper article below. Then answer the questions.

Members of Pax Christi USA have launched a Campaign for a Just US Policy for Haiti. Headed by Auxiliary Bishop Thomas Gumbleton of Detroit, they made a sidewalk protest in front of the Washington White House against military intervention in Haiti. The group announced that it intended to stage similar vigils weekly to support the peaceful return to power of President Aristide.

(*The Tablet*, 9 July 1994)

1 Research the situation in Haiti, where the President, a former priest, has recently returned home following his exile in the USA.
2 Do you think bishops should be in public protests against government?
3 Do you think it is appropriate for the Christian Church openly to criticize government? If so, what issues should it address?

'Never again one against the other, never, never, never again…never again war! It is peace, peace, that must guide the destiny of the people of all humanity.'

(Pope Paul VI to the UN, 1965)

Fighting one another is contrary to everything that Jesus stands for. One would expect therefore that Christians would be in the forefront of peace programmes, and that Christian countries would never be part of the war scene. The scandal is that religion plays as big a part in war as anything else. The issues are so complex that Church leaders seem powerless to influence their communities. A radio reporter from the blood-bath in Rwanda said that what she saw there discredited Christianity:

'There was no Christian voice at the height of the war. I saw a Catholic priest abandon what his faith meant and actually hack to death people hiding behind the altar because they were the wrong tribe.'

(August 1994)

This was, perhaps an isolated case, and there are other stories emerging of heroic priests and people. But war is brutal, and national and cultural loyalties are so strong that religion sometimes has little influence on people's behaviour. The situation in Northern Ireland is proof enough of this.

Textbooks can quickly become out of date. In the last few years, there have been great changes in the shift of power in the world and this has meant that politicians have had to rethink their policies on issues of war and peace. Everyone wants peace. But not everyone (not even Church leaders) can agree on the best way to achieve it. The chart illustrates this. It is an outline of the 'Just War Theory' and shows the way opposing sides read the situation during the Gulf War. The Pope took the view that the war was unjustified. The Archbishop of Canterbury supported the war.

It is hardly surprising that a Catholic (Jesuit) paper in Rome published a leading article maintaining that the Just War Theory is now outdated, since modern weapons unleash a violence that is quite unacceptable. The article claimed that since the conditions for a just war no longer exist, there can never any longer be a right to wage war.

THE JUST WAR THEORY: THE GULF WAR

A Just War must:	Was it justified?	
	Yes	No
● be undertaken by lawful authority	UN Security Council accepted responsibility	US President Bush anticipated the UN
● have a just cause and intention, (self-defence, restoring peace, etc.)	To free Kuwait	The real motive was to safeguard oil for the West
● be the last resort (all other ways tried)	Diplomacy was tried and a deadline given	Not long enough given for diplomacy
● have reasonable hope of success	It was short, sharp and decisive	The devastation of Iraq, and its distrust of the West, will last for years
● protect civilians (especially children, women, elderly)	Modern warfare can pinpoint accurately	Civilian casualties were enormous
● ensure the good achieved outweighs the evil of war	Freedom is the ultimate good	War has added to the problems
● guarantee the behaviour of troops	We have disciplined troops these days	Some troops always act with cruelty

REFLECTIONS

On pacifism

'All who take the sword will perish by the sword.'

(Jesus in *Matthew* 26:52)

'We do not make war on our enemies;…we gladly die confessing Christ.'

(St Justin, AD 165)

'I am a soldier of Christ, I cannot fight.'

(St Martin of Tours resigning from the Roman army in the fourth century)

On nuclear issues

Nuclear weapons must be banned. A general agreement must be reached on a suitable disarmament programme, with an effective system of mutual control.

(The encyclical *Pacem in Terris*, 1963)

The only legitimate purpose of nuclear deterrence is to prevent war…But deterrence based on balance, not as an end in itself but as a step on the way toward a progressive disarmament, may still be judged morally acceptable.

(From *CEM* summary of consensus in RC teaching)

'Ban the bomb!' The slogan which many of us shouted for decades…has quite suddenly become respectable. It is now widely whispered by serious men in blue suits, civil servants from smoke-filled corridors, treaty negotiators pale from long nights at baize-covered tables in Geneva, their mouths full of SALT, START, INF, CFE, CWC, BWC and other unchewable syllables; all are now talking about the possibility of a nuclear free-world.

(Brian Wicker in *JUSTPEACE*, July 1994)

Poverty and the arms race

The arms race is an utterly treacherous trap for humanity, and one which ensnares the poor to an intolerable degree.

(*Gaudium et Spes* 81)

The arms race does not ensure peace. Far from eliminating the causes of war, it aggravates them. Spending enormous sums to produce ever new types of weapons impedes efforts to aid needy populations, it thwarts the development of peoples.

(*Catechism of the Catholic Church*, No. 2315)

THINGS TO DO

▶ Research the following topics and make notes on each:
- pacifism
- the Just War Theory
- the nuclear debate
- the arms race
- the cost of war.

▶ List the causes of war, giving examples of actual wars.

▶ Write an article commenting on this statement by Pope John Paul II: 'Our future on this planet…depends on one single factor; humanity must make a moral about-face.'

1 WORK: ON BEHALF OF OTHERS

'Good teacher, what must I do to receive eternal life?' … 'There is one more thing you need to do. Sell all you have and give the money to the poor, and you will have riches in heaven; then come and follow me.'

(Luke 18:18,22)

This story of the rich man might give the impression that all Christians are called to give up earning money, or forbidden to take jobs which are not directly at the service of the Church. This is not so. The story says something about values. Christians interpret it to mean that whether one becomes an official in the Church or not, all must keep their eyes on Jesus to follow his value system.

In the world of work this means for a Christian:

- putting others first
- service with a smile
- generous sharing
- never exploiting others
- respect for the rights of other people
- never hurting others by greed
- respect for the whole of creation.

These are issues we have already considered in this book. The photograph shows Sr Maureen and Mrs Joan Peter working with children who have disabilities. There is not much money in such work, but much happiness.

Catholics, along with others, see work as a means for self-fulfilment and service. But it is balanced by a 'gift' of leisure, so that the person can reach fullness and wholeness: 'The glory of God is a person fully human'. Catholics have never shared the Calvinistic 'work ethic' which believed in work as a sacred duty. Calvin developed this view from texts of St Paul that praised workers and condemned the lazy (see *II Thessalonians 3:6–11*, *Ephesians 6:5–7*). Catholics put such advice alongside Jesus' word that the birds and flowers are blessed by God without having to work for it (*Matthew 6:26*).

The world of work does not escape problems. Consider these:

- unemployment
- Sunday shop openings
- discrimination in the work place
- child labour
- over-qualification for jobs
- exploitation of women.

The Catholic Church's attitude to work was expressed in some detail by Pope John Paul II in an encyclical *Laborem Exercens*. The encyclical emphasizes the priority of the workers over the suppliers of capital – a move away from former Popes who seemed to approve of a capitalist system dependent on investment, profit-making and competition. More recently, many Catholics, with other Christians, claim that a socialist system is rather closer to the Gospel. Socialism favours the community as a whole taking control of production.

THINGS TO DO

▶ Write a paragraph on each of the six problems listed above.

▶ Give one clear example for each.

▶ Name two jobs that you think a Christian would find unacceptable. Imagine you are a reporter interviewing the manager who is responsible for one of these jobs. Ask them to justify their position. Write up the interview.

Sister Maureen and Mrs Joan Peter with disabled children

2 WORK: FOR GAIN

The love of money is the root of all evil.

(1 Timothy 6:10)

Having money is neither good nor bad. Christians believe that it is greed, the love of money for selfish reasons, that is wrong. There are plenty of millionaires who enjoy their wealth and use it to help other people.

In Frinton, Essex, Stan Platt, a successful businessmen, uses his leisure and money to organize regular trips to Romania to help relieve the acute suffering there. You may know of others in your own town or parish who use their money in this way.

By contrast, there are people who exploit others, using them to make themselves rich. When newspaper barons or city speculators are convicted of fraud, we all tend to shake our heads in disbelief at such greed. But as the Churches have consistently pointed out, none of us is free from guilt in this respect. We in the North (the first world) keep the third world in the South poor. Christian Aid, CAFOD and Justice and Peace groups remind us year by year that the whole world economic system continues to make the rich richer at the expense of the poor. We have already seen something of this problem in talking about the arms race and about the incredible ability of corrupt governments to survive. The greatest problem of all is the ever-escalating debt incurred by poor countries through IMF (International Monetary Fund) and World Bank loans.

At local level, Catholics need to be reminded of their personal responsibility for the sharing of the earth's resources. Schools and parishes often mount campaigns that suggest how ordinary people can help; e.g. by:

- buying coffee at realistic prices for the growers
- boycotting multinational organizations that exploit the poor
- writing to MPs when government policy is for self-interest
- asking the government to increase overseas aid.

What is your school doing?

Luke 18:25

REFLECTION

Has capitalism with its market system triumphed? To some extent, yes. But within the capitalist system, the poor do not fare well. The system exists for the capitalists in the centres of power…Before (in the days of slavery) the poor felt oppressed but they had hopes. Today, they continue oppressed and, because oppression gets worse, many have lost hope.

(Leonardo Boff)

THINGS TO DO

▶ What is capitalism?

▶ What is Leonardo Boff saying about this system?

▶ What do you think we could go without in Britain so that the government could increase overseas aid? Prepare a five-minute talk to give to the class.

I pray that they may all be one. Father! May they be in us, just as you are in me and I am in you.

(John 17:21)

A Catholic mother wrote recently:

'Mum, are we Christians?' It was Tom, my middle son, who asked the question. Tom was then nine years old; he had served at the altar for four years and had made his First Communion two years before. He had been brought up – quite well, I assumed to that moment – on angels, saints, holy water and goodnight prayers. And then he asked something like that. Had I failed? Would I have to start again from scratch?

Roman Catholics are Christians. Not all Christians are Roman Catholics. You will have discovered in this book that on most issues Christians are happily in agreement. Yet they are also separated and, for many, this is a scandal. The community at Taizé in France prays constantly that the future will bring unity. This movement is called **ecumenism**.

Never resign yourself to the scandal of the separation of Christians – all so readily professing love for their neighbour, yet remaining divided. Make the unity of Christ's Body your passionate concern.

(Taizé Community)

Here are two hopeful signs for the future.

1 The following text from the *Inter Faith Network* for the United Kingdom was published in *Briefing*, a publication of the Roman Catholic Bishops' Conference.

In Britain today, people of many different faiths and beliefs live side by side. The opportunity lies before us to work together to build a society rooted in the values we treasure. But this society can only be built on a sure foundation of mutual respect, openness and trust. This means finding ways to live our lives of faith with integrity, and allowing others to do so too. Our different religious traditions offer us many resources for this, and teach us the importance of good relationships characterized by honesty, compassion and generosity of spirit. Together, listening and responding with openness and respect, we can move forward to work in ways that acknowledge genuine differences, but build on shared hopes and values.

2 The following extract is about the street children of Rio.

In Rio, a group of Christians was working with street children. Every day boys from the street got together at one spot to chat, to discuss their problems and to share their fears and anger with one another. Many came regularly. The church people consisted of a Catholic priest, a Methodist, a priest of the Umbanda cult, a Presbyterian, and a young Lutheran pastor.

One day one of the boys said: 'I would like to be baptized.'
'In which church, then?' asked the Catholic.
'Which church? In ours here, of course.'
'But to which church building would you like to go?'
'Building? No, to our church, here on the street. I want to be baptized here among us.'

The Methodist said he couldn't issue such a certificate. The Catholic thought it wouldn't be possible to perform jointly with the man from the Umbanda religion. The boy stuck by his wish.

Finally, the pastor organized the necessary things: he laid a board over two crates and filled an old boot with water for flowers, which the children provided. The Catholic brought along a candle.

The baptism took place on the street, in the name of Jesus Christ.

(Dorothee Soelle, *Celebrating Resistance*, 1993)

Street children who only know the 'church on the streets'

Looking back through this book one thing is certain: you will have found all the texts and wordy paragraphs about religious beliefs less interesting than the people. You need to have understood the words, but it is far more important that you remember the people. The Catholic Church is the people, not the building or the teachings or the leaders – but the ordinary people baptized at the font or in the Rio street.

'Go then to all people everywhere and make them my disciples: baptize them in the name of the Father, the Son, and the Holy Spirit, and teach them to obey everything I have commanded you. And I will be with you always, to the end of the age.'

(Matthew 28:19–20)

The playwright Dennis Potter, who died from cancer in 1994, said these words in his last interview with broadcaster Melvyn Bragg on TV's Channel 4. Discuss them.

'I'm almost serene. I can celebrate life. Below my window there's an apple tree in blossom. It's white. And looking at it – instead of saying, "Oh, that's a nice blossom" – now, looking at it through the window, I see the whitest, frothiest, blossomest blossom that there ever could be. The nowness of everything is absolutely wondrous. If you see the present tense – boy, do you see it, and boy, do you celebrate it.'

(Dennis Potter, July 1994)

SOME IMPORTANT ADDRESSES

These are the addresses of organizations mentioned in this book. When writing to them try to send one letter from the whole class and always enclose a SAE.

Bourne Trust
(Catholic service to prisoners)
Lincoln House
Kennington Park
1–3 Brixton Road
London SW9 6DE

Catholic Agency for Overseas Development
(CAFOD)
2 Romero Close
Stockwell Road
London SW9 9TY

The Catholic Children's Society
(Crusade of Rescue)
Dept LT
St Charles Square
London W10 6EJ

Catholic Housing Aid Society
(CHAS)
189a Old Brompton Road
London SW5 0AR

Catholic Institute for International Relations
(CIIR)
Unit 3,
Canonbury Yard
190a New North Road
London N1 7BJ

Catholic Marriage Advisory Council
(CMAC)
1 Blythe Mews
Blythe Road
London W14 0NW

Catholic Truth Society
(CTS)
38–40 Eccleston Square
London SW1Y 1PD

LIFE
Life House
Newbold Terrace
Royal Leamington Spa
CV32 4EA

Pax Christi
9 Henry Road
London N4 2LH

QUEST
BM Box 2585
London WC1N 3XX

Shelter
157 Waterloo Road
London SE1 8XF

SPUC
7 Tufton Street
Westminster
London SW1P 3QN

St Vincent de Paul Society
24 George Street
London W1H 5RB

GLOSSARY

Absolution   Forgiveness. The priest's assurance, in the sacrament of penance, that sins are forgiven.

Advent   Coming. A period of four weeks of preparation for the coming of Christ at Christmas, and at the end of time.

Altar   Raised up. The raised table used for the celebration of Mass.

Anointing   Sacrament in which the sign of the cross is made with oil on sick people, and prayers are said for their healing.

Annunciation   The angel's announcement, in the Gospel story, that the child about to be born to Mary would be Son of God.

Apostle   Sent. The title of the twelve men whom Jesus sent to preach the Gospel.

Ascension   Going up. The feast, 40 days after Easter, which celebrates Jesus' return to his Father in heaven.

Ash Wednesday   The first day of Lent, when ashes are distributed as a sign of penance.

Assumption   Taken up. Catholics believe that what happened to Jesus at Easter will happen to them too, and has already happened to Mary, the first of all Christians.

Baptism   Sacrament in which water is poured on to people as a sign of their new life in Christ, and their becoming members of the Christian Church.

Beatitudes   The blessings, or true happiness, which Jesus surprisingly said belongs to the world's unfortunates: the poor, the hungry and the persecuted.

Benediction   Blessing with the consecrated host given in some churches at evening service.

Bishop   Supervisor. The person appointed in each district to lead and teach the Christian community.

Blessed Sacrament   Consecrated hosts kept for later communion (see **Tabernacle**)

Canonization   The official declaration that a person has led a saintly life and is now with God.

Chalice   Cup, usually a precious one, used to hold the wine at Mass.

Christ   Anointed. A Greek form of the Hebrew *messiah*, used of the deliverer whom God was expected to send. The followers of Jesus gave him this title.

Christmas   The feast (Mass) on 25 December celebrating the birth of Jesus Christ.

Church   The community of Christians, or the building where they meet.

Ciborium   Small box. A lidded container for consecrated hosts, kept in the tabernacle and used for communion.

Communion of saints   See Saints. Christians believe that all those, past or present, who are close to God, are close to each other, and form a communion or community.

Confession   The older name for the sacrament of Penance which emphasized the reciting (confessing) of sins committed.

Confirmation   Sacrament in which adults confirm their infant baptism before a bishop.

Consecration   Making sacred. The ceremony by which people or certain things (a church, for example, or an altar, or the bread and wine at Mass) are solemnly dedicated to the service of God.

Contrition   Sorrow for sins that have been committed.

Corpus Christi   More recently, *Corpus et Sanguis Christi*: Body and Blood of Christ. The summer feastday which celebrates Jesus' gift of the Eucharist to his Church.

Creed   Belief. A statement of what people believe.

Crucifix   A representation of the death Jesus died, nailed to a cross.

Deacon   Servant. A person ordained to help bishops and priests in their work.

Easter   The springtime feast celebrating God's raising of Jesus from death.

Ecumenism   Worldwide. The movement towards unity by the separated Churches.

Epistle   Letter. One of the 21 letters written by the first Christian leaders, now included in the New Testament.

Eucharist   Thanksgiving. One of the words used for the Mass (and especially for the consecrated bread and wine), which emphasizes gratitude to God for the gift of Jesus.

Evangelist   One of the four writers of the *evangel* or good news known as the Gospel.

Extreme Unction   Last anointing. See **Anointing**.

Font   Fountain. The basin in which the water used for baptism is kept.

Genuflection   Going down on one knee as a mark of respect in church.

Good Friday   The Friday before Easter, when the death of Jesus is most solemnly commemorated.

Gospel   The Old English words *god spel* mean 'good news'. They refer to what was done by Jesus, and to the four written accounts of this.

Grace   Free Gift. The undeserved goodness with which God loves people and draws them to himself. The word is also used for the Christian prayer of thanks before and after meals.

Hail Mary   The opening words of the angel's greeting to Mary (*Luke 1:28*) now used as a prayer.

Heaven   Where God is.

Hell   Where God is not.

Hierarchy   Sacred Rule. The word used of bishops as leaders ('rulers') of the Christian community.

Holy Communion   The receiving of the consecrated bread and wine at Mass, a sign of people's union with Christ, and with each other.

Holy Days   A number of weekdays in the year on which, in Christian countries, work stops (hence the word *holiday*) in order to allow everyone to celebrate religious feasts such as Ascension, Assumption, etc.

Holy Ghost, Spirit   The word used by the New Testament to speak of the presence and power of God with which Jesus was filled, and which he promised his followers would share. In theological language this is referred to as the 'Third Person of the Blessed Trinity'.

Holy Orders   See **Order**.

Holy Water   Water that has been blessed, and which people use to make the sign of the cross on themselves to remind them of their baptism.

Holy Week   The week before Easter, in which the events that led to Jesus' death are recalled.

Host   Victim. The word used for the bread which at Mass becomes a sacrament of Christ's body, broken on the cross.

Icon   Image. A religious painting or mosaic in a style which tries to make visible the invisible world of God and the saints.

Immaculate Conception   Conceived without stain. The Catholic belief that, in view of the role she had to play, the life of Jesus' mother Mary was without sin from the very beginning.

Incarnation   In the Body. The biblical teaching that the mystery of God is to be met in the lives of people of flesh and blood. For Christians, the uniquely supreme instance of this is the life of the man Jesus.

Incense   A sweet-smelling spice whose smoke is used to give a sense of celebration in religious ceremonies.

Infallibility   Catholics believe that God preserves the Church from serious error. Without this gift it could not faithfully hand on the Word of God. It is exercised when solemn statements are made by the bishops assembled in council, or by the Pope speaking in their name.

Kyrie eleison   Lord have mercy. The Greek words Christians use at the beginning of Mass to express their confidence in Christ, whose servants they are.

Lectern   The desk from which the Bible is read at Mass.

Lectionary   The collection of Bible passages chosen for readings at Mass through the year.

Lent   Spring. A period of 40 days of penitential preparation for Easter.

Liturgy   Public service. The official services of the Church, as distinct from private devotions.

Magisterium   Teaching. The whole Church fulfils Christ's command to 'teach all nations', but the word is mostly used of the official teaching done by bishops.

Marriage, matrimony   The sacrament in which the love of a husband and wife becomes a sign of God's love for all people.

Mass   Sending. The eucharistic service of readings and holy communion, recalling and re-enacting the Last Supper of Jesus. The word with which the congregation was dismissed (Mass) has become the name of the whole service, which people are sent to live out in their daily lives.

Maundy   Command. The name given to the Thursday before Easter, when Jesus gave his disciples the command to serve each other.

Missal   The book containing the prayers and directives (rubrics) that are laid down for celebrating Mass.

Monks and nuns   Men and women who have deliberately given up property and marriage in order to be free to serve the community.

Mother of God   A title which Christians give to Mary, the mother of Jesus.

New Testament, Old Testament Testament means 'agreement'. Jews believe that God made a binding agreement with them through their leader Moses. Christians believe that this agreement was renewed and extended to all people through Jesus. The 73 books which tell of this testament form the Bible.

Order, ordination The sacrament in which the 'ordering' of the followers of Jesus is ensured by the appointment of ministers to serve the Christian community: bishops, priests and deacons.

Original sin The Hebrew word *Adam* means the human race. The sin of Adam is the complex network of human sin which no one entering the world can escape, and from which it is the work of Christ to save the human race.

Palm Sunday The Sunday before Easter when palms are carried in memory of Jesus' last entry into Jerusalem.

Paraclete Counsellor. A title given to the presence of Christ in his Spirit, continuing to counsel his friends.

Passion Suffering. A general word used for the series of events which led to the death of Jesus.

Penance One of the seven sacraments in which assurance is given to penitents that their sins are forgiven. The word is also used for the prayers they agree to pray afterwards.

Pentecost The fiftieth day after Easter, when the disciples of Jesus powerfully experienced the Spirit of the risen Christ present among them.

Pope Father. The title given to the bishop of Rome, as the father of the worldwide Catholic family.

Priest Elder. Those among the 'older' members of the Christian community chosen by bishops to help them in their task.

Pulpit A raised platform in church used for preaching.

Purgatory Cleansing. The belief that those who die need to be cleansed of their sinfulness before they are fit to enter the presence of God.

Pyx Box. A small container for carrying a host to the housebound for holy communion.

Real Presence The Catholic teaching that in the Eucharist there is a presence of Christ that is real and independent of the faith of those who receive it.

Reconciliation Another name for the sacrament of Penance, in which sinners find themselves reconciled and at peace with God.

Redemption Buying back. The work of Jesus in setting people free is compared to the price paid to set people free from slavery.

Relics Remains. All people love to have a memento to remind them of friends who have died. The Christian veneration of relics of the saints is part of this love. It can be (and has been) overdone at times.

Religious order See **Monks and nuns**.

Resurrection The Old Testament expressed the hope that the life of God's friends would not end at death; they would be raised from death on Judgement Day. Christians believe this hope was fulfilled in Jesus at the first Easter, and will be shared by all his friends at the end of time.

Roman Catholic Christians who owe loyalty to the bishop of Rome, whom they call the Pope.

Rosary A devotion to Mary, mother of Jesus, in which the prayer 'Hail Mary' is recited 50 times while beads are counted off, and Gospel stories are meditated on.

Sacrament Sacred sign. Various signs which point to God, and lead people to him, and bring them into the presence of God. For Christians, the word applies first and foremost to Jesus as the Sacrament of God; and his work continues to be made present not only in Baptism and Eucharist, but also (for Catholics) in Confirmation, Penance, Anointing, Orders and Marriage.

Saints The Jesus-like figures throughout history, whose example Christians try to follow.

Sign of the cross The tracing of a cross, from head to chest and shoulder to shoulder, which Christians use as a reminder of the love of Jesus.

Sin Anything which harms or destroys our friendship with God or with others.

Stations of the cross Stopping places. The pictures on the walls of a church at which people stop to meditate on Jesus' journey to his death on a cross.

Statues Pictures of Christ and the saints have been used as devotional aids from the earliest times. Statues are simply pictures in 3D.

Tabernacle A draped box or container in church, in which bread consecrated at Mass is reserved for taking to the housebound later. It is marked by a continuously burning light, and acknowledged by bowing or genuflecting in its direction.

Trans-substantiation   Change of substance. A theological explanation of the presence of Christ in the Eucharist, which continues to look like bread and wine. The outward appearances (colour, taste, etc.) remain, but the inner reality (substance) is changed into the body and blood of Christ.

Trinity   Three-in-one. A shorthand way in which Christians acknowledge that for them the word 'God' is not reserved for the Father and Creator of all things, but extends to the Jesus in whose life that God was manifested, and to the Spirit in whom Christ is still present among them.

Unction   See **Anointing**.

Vatican   The part of Rome in which St Peter is buried, and which has become the headquarters of the Catholic Church.

Vestments   Clothing. The ceremonial clothes worn by ministers for religious services.

Virgin birth   The story of Jesus' birth emphasizes the belief that he is not the result of human merit or effort, but in every way God's gracious gift to the world, the Godsend of all time.

Vocation   Calling. Christians believe that the way of life they have chosen is a response to a call of God.

Whitsun   The name sometimes given to Pentecost, after the white robes worn by those coming to be baptized on this 'birthday' of the Church.

INDEX